W0254522

BEASTS OF THE ANCIENT WORLD

A KIDS' GUIDE TO MYTHICAL CREATURES, FROM THE SPHINX TO THE MINOTAUR, DRAGONS TO BAKU.

WRITTEN BY MARCHELLA WARD
ILLUSTRATED BY ASIA ORLANDO

Editor Satu Hämeenaho-Fox
Designer Lisa Robb

Project Editor Rosie Peet
Senior Designer Nathan Martin
Production Editor Siu Yin Chan
Senior Production Controller Louise Minihane
Senior Acquisitions Editor Katy Flint
Managing Art Editor Vicky Short
Publishing Director Mark Searle

For Elsa and Paws, my household beasts.

First published in Great Britain in 2023 by
Dorling Kindersley Limited
DK, One Embassy Gardens, 8 Viaduct Gardens,
London SW11 7BW

The authorised representative in the EEA is
Dorling Kindersley Verlag GmbH. Arnulfstr. 124,
80636 Munich, Germany

10 9 8 7 6 5 4 3 2 1
001–331791–Sept/2023

A CIP catalogue record for this book
is available from the British Library.
ISBN: 978-0-2415-6907-8

Printed and bound in Slovakia

DK would like to thank Sophie Dryburgh for editorial assistance.

For the curious
www.dk.com

MIX
Paper | Supporting responsible forestry
FSC www.fsc.org FSC™ C018179

This book was made with Forest Stewardship Council™ certified paper – one small step in DK's commitment to a sustainable future.
For more information go to www.dk.com/our-green-pledge

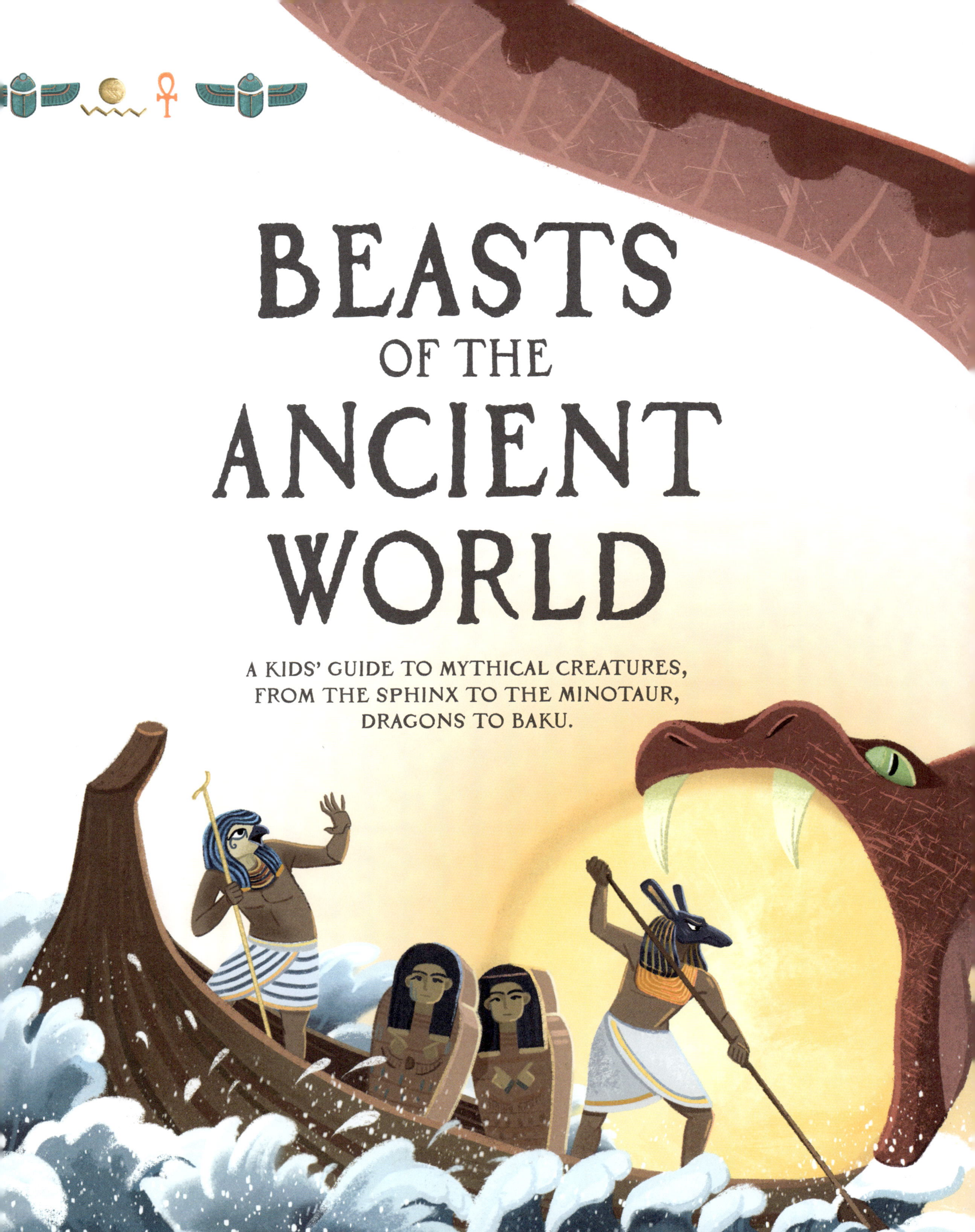

BEASTS OF THE ANCIENT WORLD

A KIDS' GUIDE TO MYTHICAL CREATURES, FROM THE SPHINX TO THE MINOTAUR, DRAGONS TO BAKU.

CONTENTS

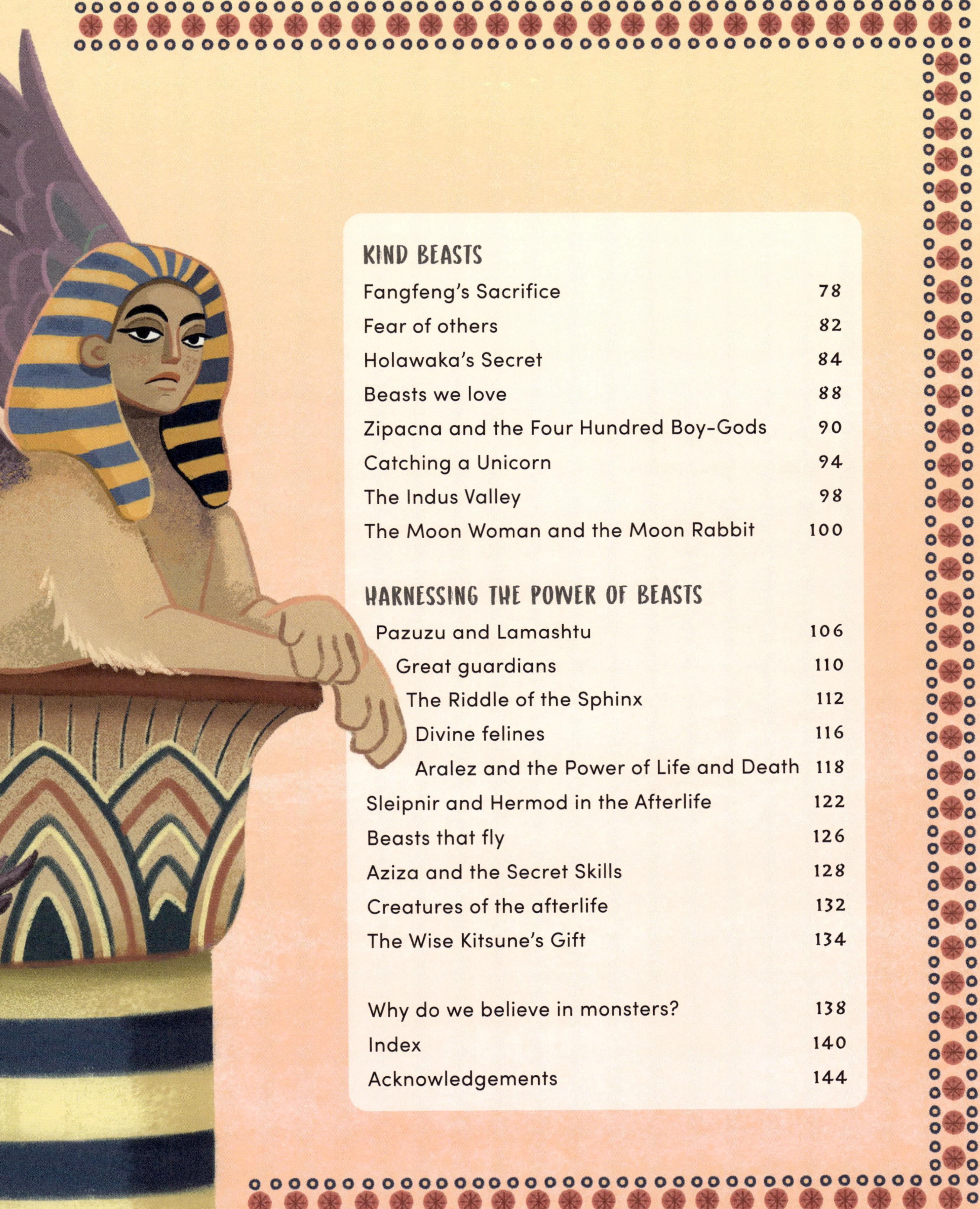

KIND BEASTS

HARNESSING THE POWER OF BEASTS

LIVING AMONG BEASTS

The most common type of story told about monsters goes like this: a brave human hero tracks down a monster who has been frightening other, less powerful humans. The human defeats the monster, usually by killing it, though sometimes by scaring it away so that it never comes back. The other humans celebrate their hero for this feat. But stories are not always so well behaved. The brave human will sometimes decide not to kill the monster. They will see that they were wrong to have thought that the monster was fierce and cruel. The human will learn that their behaviour needed to change.

Defeating monsters in these stories means much more than cutting off their hundred heads with a sword, or shooting them through the heart with a burning arrow. It means learning to work together, and to help each other to conquer things we could not conquer alone. It means recognising when something is dishonest, or unfair, and speaking out against it. It means being kind to the Earth, and treating the natural world as our friend and not as something we can use for our own benefit. It means understanding that difference is not something to be scared of – that sometimes the best thing to do is to learn from those who live very different lives to our own. That we shouldn't call someone a 'monster' until we understand their whole story.

The stories about monsters in this book come from all over the ancient world. I have pieced them together from scraps of stories told to me by other people, or stories that I found in old books, or on fragments of pottery or papyrus in dusty libraries. There are other – more recent – stories about monsters that I have not told in this book. You see, the word 'monster' has a dangerous history. It has been a label that has sometimes been used to insult certain groups of people. When European colonisers first went to the African continent, and to the places that became the Americas, for instance, they said that they had found monsters there. They spread lies about how the people there had three eyes instead of two, or ate their food through the tops of their heads, or walked on their hands.

The stories they told were not true, but there was a particular purpose to telling them. The colonisers wanted to take these people's lands and resources for themselves. And calling these people 'monsters' instead of 'humans' meant that they could treat them as less than human. It also meant that it was easy to argue that these people should be 'defeated', like the mythical beasts in ancient stories. By telling these ancient stories again, we can unravel this history. We can stop these dangerous uses of the word 'monster' in its tracks, and read the stories in different ways. We can read them as proof that all humans, whatever shapes their bodies have and however their own unique bodies work, are equal. And as proof that being cruel to others is never the solution to being afraid.

These stories remind us that things are never really as simple as brave human defeats monster. Far more often than they show us brave humans defeating monsters, these ancient tales show us even braver humans learning to live among them.

A WORLD OF CREATURES

From terrifying demons to kind, friendly unicorns, mythical beasts are found in stories from all over the ancient world. People told these stories around fires, at the dinner table, and at bedtime from ancient Greece to ancient China and from the Caribbean to what is now New Zealand. Sometimes ancient storytellers were inspired by real-life animals that they saw in the world around them. The mythical creatures in these stories moved around the whole world as migration, colonialism, trade, travel, wars, and friendships carried them far away from the places they were first imagined.

Sleipnir
Norse
Medusa
Greece
Aralez
Armenia
Sphinx
Greece
Buffalo demon
India
Pegasus
Greece
Kitsune
Japan
Fangfeng
China
Mami Wata
West Africa
Apep
Egypt
Pazuzu
Mesopotamia
Unicorn
India
Tiyanak
Philippines
Aman Doger
Nubia
Moon Rabbit
East Asia
Aziza
Dahomey
Holowaka
Ethiopia
N
W
E
S
Ponaturi
Maori

OUR WORST FEARS

What is it that you are most afraid of? Being lost on your own in the woods? Deep, dark water with something scary lurking just beneath the surface? Being stolen away from your family? Beasts are a tool that we use to tell these stories. They help us to imagine the things that scare us most, and they give us a way to talk about them with other people. We need these stories so that we can warn others – so that no one has to make the same mistake twice. And these stories are not just about terrifying monsters and dangerous beasts, they are about humans too. In them we see just how strong and courageous people can be when they are protecting the ones they love, and standing up for the ideas they believe in.

THE GIRL WHO MET THE LOOGAROO

In every house on every island, parents told their children not to stay out late at night after it was dark or the Loogaroo might get them. Most of the children were too afraid of the Loogaroo to do anything other than obey their parents. But in one house, on one island, there lived a young girl who was not like the others. She wanted to know what kind of monster this Loogaroo was.

Night after night the girl would ask, and night after night her mother would have no answer. Eventually, her grandmother knocked on the door. She took her granddaughter aside and told her everything that she knew about the Loogaroo, while her mother took a much-needed nap.

No one knew exactly what the Loogaroo was, her grandmother told her, because no one had ever met the monster and survived. "On our island," she said, "people say that the Loogaroo is an old woman who has made a deal with the demon who lives in the silk cotton tree, and steals children for him. She removes her skin at night so that she can slip through cracks in the walls without being seen." Across the sea, on the island over the horizon people said that the Loogaroo turned into a wolf at night and kidnapped any children it could find.

The little girl listened quietly, but it did not stop her from feeling curious. After her grandmother had tucked her into bed and left for the night, she decided to go in search of this monster. She grabbed a handful of cassava flour from the storage jar and a pinch of salt – so that if she were to get lost she would at least be able to make cassava bread. Then she left the house.

She walked all the way up to the crossroads just outside of the town, where she had seen an old woman earlier that day gathering herbs underneath a silk cotton tree. The woman had been grinding the herbs up with a pestle and mortar and putting them into her pockets. When the little girl arrived at the bottom of the tree, the old woman was nowhere to be seen... but then the girl noticed something. The old woman's mortar was still there, but when the girl looked inside it she saw no herbs. Instead, a thin, wrinkled skin filled the mortar. It looked almost like the old woman had shed her skin. A shiver of fear made its way slowly up the little girl's spine.

The girl turned to run but a ball of fire shot out of the night sky. It sped up, going faster and faster until it was turning circles around her. The girl felt dread as she realised that she could not run fast enough. She stopped and dropped to the ground. "I know who you are!" she said, raising her head. "You're the Loogaroo, and now that you have caught me you will take me away from my family and feed me to the demon who lives in the silk cotton tree!" The ball of fire burst into even brighter flames close to the girl's face. She searched in her pockets for a weapon to defend herself, but found only the handful of cassava flour. She threw it in the direction of the Loogaroo and covered her face with her hands.

At that moment something surprising happened. The ball of fire flew down low over the cassava flour. It hovered there slowly for a while. You see, there was something the girl's grandmother had not told her. Whenever the Loogaroo encountered a pile of grains, she could not stop herself from counting them. Even if there were thousands of grains in front of her, she would pick up and count each and every one. After she had hovered there for what felt like an eternity, the Loogaroo sped away back to the silk cotton tree. She was heading for the mortar containing the old woman's skin.

The little girl jumped up. Would the same trick work twice? She threw the salt at the Loogaroo, but it landed in the mortar, covering the old woman's skin. The Loogaroo howled. She was trying to put her skin back on and return to her human form so that she could pick up each of the grains of flour. But her human form did not fit her.

The salt had dried out her skin so much it could no longer stretch back over her limbs. In a flash she transformed back into a ball of fire and flew off into the night. No one saw the Loogaroo on the island ever again.

PERSEUS AND MEDUSA

The young hero Perseus had lost count of how many times he and his mother Danae had been in danger. For example, they had been thrown out to sea in a wooden chest by King Acrisius, who was scared of Perseus's strength. While the chest was battered by the waves, Perseus and Danae had prayed to Poseidon, god of the sea, for what seemed like an eternity. They survived. But they had washed up on the shore of King Polydectes, who separated the two of them and enslaved Danae, putting her to work in his house. Perseus had searched for days and days for his mother, until eventually he had found her sweeping the floors in the king's palace, and they were reunited.

This time Perseus was not sure that he and Danae would ever be safe again. King Polydectes had promised that he would free her only if Perseus brought him an impossible gift: the head of the gorgon, Medusa. This was a monster who looked almost human except that she had wings, and poisonous snakes on her head instead of hair. She could turn people to stone just by looking at them. King Polydectes did not think Perseus would return alive.

The first thing that Perseus did was say a prayer to the goddess Athena, who appeared to him in full battle armour. She told him to find the Hesperides. These nymphs lived in the place where the Sun went when it set. But Athena had not told Perseus where to

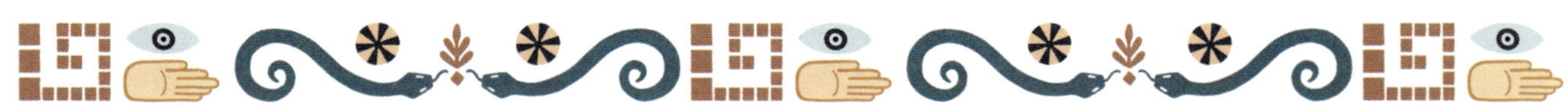

find the Hesperides, so he had to go to where the Graiai lived and try to find out. The Graiai were three sisters who were older than time itself and knew everything there was to know. They shared one eye and one tooth between them, and took turns using them.

When Perseus arrived in the cave of the Graiai, the sisters passed the eye between them to take a look at him. As soon as his own eyes had adjusted to the darkness, Perseus snatched the eye from mid-air as one of the sisters threw it to the other. He held it out of their reach and said, "I will only give this eye back if you tell me where to find the Hesperides!" The Graiai groaned, but they did as Perseus had asked. They told him to head west, and not to stop until he came to the place where the Sun set. Perseus threw back the eye and started walking west.

As he walked, the Sun began to sink in the sky. In the distance he heard the clear voices of young women singing, and eventually he was close enough to see seven nymphs. The Hesperides lived in an orchard where there were golden apples on the trees and where everything glowed the orange colour of sunset. After Perseus told them his story, they immediately agreed to help him. They gave him a sack to carry Medusa's head in, then they showed him the gifts that the gods had told them to keep safe for him. From the king of the gods, Zeus, they gave him a sword so strong that it could cut through anything, and a bronze helmet that made its wearer invisible. From Athena they gave him a shield that was polished until it sparkled and reflected more clearly than any mirror. Then they gave him winged sandals from Hermes, the messenger of the gods. Perseus took these gifts, and listened carefully to their instructions. Then he set off.

Perseus had been walking for several days when he began to notice something strange about his surroundings. With every two or three steps he took he would pass a statue made of stone. The statues looked like they were in pain, or trying to defend themselves. Some of them had their arms raised in front of their faces, and others twisted their bodies away or had their mouths open in horror. Perseus carried on walking. Soon he was surrounded by hundreds of these strange statues. It was then that he heard the hissing of snakes, and realised that he had arrived at the cave where Medusa lived.

Although the snakes on her head were awake and hissing at Perseus, Medusa was asleep and snoring loudly. Perseus put on the bronze helmet so that he was invisible. He held Athena's shield so that he could see Medusa's reflection but not risk looking directly at her and turning to stone like all the statues he had passed on his way into the cave. Then he took the sword in his hand and, as quietly as he could, tiptoed over to where Medusa was sleeping. He sliced her head from her neck and then – once the snakes had all stopped hissing – he slid it into the sack that the Hesperides had woven. Then using the sandals that Hermes had told the nymphs to give to him, he sped off. He gave Medusa's head to King Polydectes who kept his promise and freed Danae. King Polydectes could not believe what Perseus had been able to do for his mother.

Terracotta Medusa 6th century BCE

Strangely, the ancient Greeks liked decorating their homes with terrifying images of Medusa. This grinning one was used to cover the end of a row of tiles on a roof.

MONSTROUS WOMEN

Throughout history, women who did not conform to men's expectations about how they should look or behave were said to be monsters. Refusing to get married, living alone (or in groups of other women), dressing in unusual ways or getting angry rather than staying silent were all things that raised suspicions that a woman was a witch or a monster. For this reason, the monsters that we meet in stories from the ancient world are more often described as female than any other gender.

Odysseus versus the monsters

In the *Odyssey*, an ancient Greek poem, the hero Odysseus must defeat an array of monsters in order to make his way safely home. Some of the most famous monsters in Greek mythology are in this poem. Odysseus has to escape Scylla, who has the upper body of a woman and the lower body of a sea monster, with three fierce dogs around her waist. Odysseus also meets the sirens, who are part-birds and part-women. They sing a song so beautiful that it lures sailors towards them and they crash their ships into the rocks. Odysseus puts beeswax in his sailors' ears so they can't hear the bewitching song. Almost every monster Odysseus meets on his journey is female.

Deer Woman

Many Indigenous American groups tell the story of the Deer Woman. This spirit takes the form of a beautiful woman who has deer hooves for feet. One story tells of a young man who leaves his community, meets the Deer Woman and falls in love with her. He does not notice her feet and is unaware that she is a magical spirit. She leads him away from his family and community, and he stays under her spell, forgetting to hunt or eat, and eventually dies. These stories are told to remind young men of their responsibilities to their families and communities. The legends of the Deer Woman remind those who hear the story to be vigilant, as not everyone may be who they appear to be – in body, mind, or spirit.

Dangerous mermaids

Stories of creatures that are half-fish, half-woman, were told throughout the ancient world – appearing first in ancient Syria almost 3,000 years ago. The Ancient Brazilian mythology of the Tupi and Guarani people tells the story of Iara, a mermaid with green hair who had the tail of a dolphin. In these stories Iara would lure men out to sea where she would drown them. In Africa, the mermaid Iemanjá, mother of all of the Yoruba spirits, could be similarly dangerous. She is the protector of women, but when someone makes her angry she can also send floods in revenge.

Snake wives

The Hindu God Krishna once fought a hundred-headed serpent called Kaliya who was poisoning a river. Kaliya managed to coil himself around Krishna so tightly that it seemed like he might strangle him. But Krishna grew to ten times his normal size. Krishna was about to kill Kaliya when the creature's many half-human, half-snake wives appeared and begged him not to kill their husband. Krishna agreed to a truce: he would let Kaliya live if he promised to leave the river forever and stay away from humans.

Blood-thirsty demon

Tataka was an Asuri, a female demon who appeared in the Hindu epic poem the *Ramayana*, written around 650–350 BCE. She roamed the forest, looking for a man called Agastya so she could kill him. At first Tataka seems like just a bloodythirsty monster, but she had a reason for being so angry with Agastya: he had put a curse on her husband, which killed him. Vengeful demons like Tataka were loud and scary. They showed everyone around exactly how angry they were and why they wanted to seek revenge.

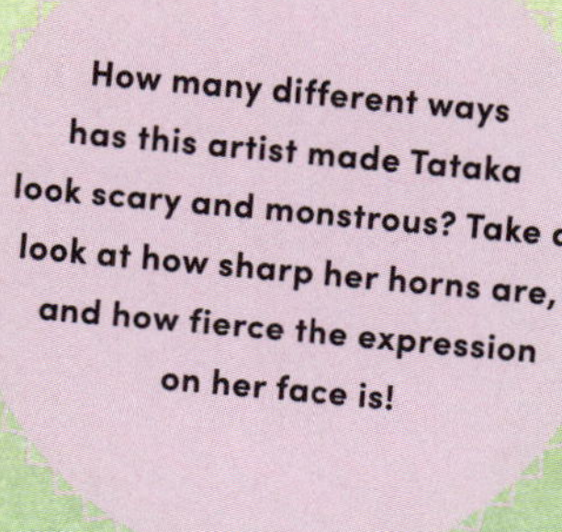

THE MONSTER OF THE NILE

In ancient Nubia, children learned early in their childhoods not to go near to the river Nile after dark. People said that a dangerous monster named Aman Doger lived there. They said that at night he would come out and suck on the nose of any human that he could find, until they died because they were unable to breathe.

At every holiday festival, the people who lived by the banks of the river would leave gifts for Aman Doger so that he would not be angry that he had been left out of the party or celebration. And sometimes Aman Doger would give the humans something in return. There were people who said that they could see the future because Aman Doger had dragged them into the Nile one night and given them their powers – but hardly anyone believed them.

It was when Alara met one of these fortune-tellers who claimed to have been given magical powers by Aman Doger that she decided to find out for herself. Like all the other children in Nubia she knew that she should not go down to the river after dark, but her curiosity got the better of her. On the bank she could see the bowls and cups full of food and drinks that the cooks of her village had left out for Aman Doger. The food was still warm and Alara thought about taking a bite herself, but she decided not to because she did not want Aman Doger to be angry with her. A few steps further down

the bank Alara saw a small pile of dates and gold coins – one of the families in the village must have welcomed a new baby, and left the usual offerings to Aman Doger to convince him not to harm their child. She put a few of the dates in her pocket in case she got hungry later on.

Mummy, 1st century
The ancient people who lived along the Nile were fascinated by creatures that could live both on land and in water, such as crocodiles. This crocodile was mummified and put in a tomb.

Alara approached the bend in the river where the water was at its deepest, and crouched down at the edge. At first she could only see her own reflection because the water was so dark. But she kept on staring into its depths until she thought she could see something moving in the mud at the bottom of the river. Two bright red dots stared back at her and it was only when the dots started to grow larger and larger that she realised that these were the eyes of Aman Doger – and that they were coming towards her!

Alara started to run but it was too late. Aman Doger could move much faster in the water than Alara could on land. And to make things worse, Aman Doger was almost invisible, blending in perfectly with the mud that lined the banks of the Nile. If Alara had been able to see Aman Doger, she would have seen legs like the legs of a donkey, enormous ears and a long tail. She would have noticed that two red eyes balanced one on top of the other.

Aman Doger leapt out of the water and attached himself to Alara with his sticky grip. He opened his mouth to wrap his lips around her nose and stop her from breathing – just as she had been warned about in the stories people had told her. The creature and the girl were about the same size but he was many times stronger. He brought his face closer and closer to Alara's – and it was at that precise moment that Alara remembered the dates.

There was nothing Aman Doger loved more than dates, not even killing humans, which was his second favourite thing. Alara pulled one of the dates from her pocket. It was too dark to see but Aman Doger sniffed the air hungrily.

Alara threw the fruit into the river and Aman Doger's whole body lurched towards it with such force that Alara fell backwards into the sand. The date sank down to the bottom of the river and Aman Doger dived in after it. Alara did not wait to find out what happened next. She ran.

Alara did not stop running until she was safely home with the door closed behind her. Her heart was racing. Suddenly she understood how those who met Aman Doger could be so terrified that they died from fear alone. Alara would never know whether being kidnapped by Aman Doger really gave you magical powers, like the fortune-tellers in the village claimed. She would never risk meeting Aman Doger again. But now she knew exactly why you shouldn't go near the river at night.

ANCIENT NUBIA

Nubia is a region in ancient Africa that runs from modern-day Egypt to Sudan along the river Nile. One of the earliest ancient African cultures – the Kerma Kingdom – ruled over this region more than four thousand years ago. It was conquered many time, by the ancient Egyptians, then by the Kingdom of Kush, and, in the 4th century CE, the Ethiopian Kingdom of Aksum. The people of ancient Nubia were famous for being extremely talented craftspeople and artists, as we can see from looking at their art and jewellery.

Animal gods

The people of ancient Nubia shared some of their gods with the people of ancient Egypt – including the god Amun. Amun often appeared to humans in the form of different animals, and especially in the form of a ram. This golden amulet showing a ram would have been worn as a necklace by one of the kings of Kush.

Nubia and Egypt

The ancient Egyptians were the neighbours of the ancient Nubians. Their relationship must have been difficult at some points in their history. Egypt wanted Nubia's natural resources – especially gold, ebony, and ivory – and took control of the region until they were defeated by the Kingdom of Kush. There are also signs of much friendlier connections between Egypt and Nubia, though. The tomb of Rekhmire, who was a governor of the city of Thebes in Egypt, is decorated with images of Nubian people bringing him animals – like a giraffe and a monkey – as gifts. This shows that even though the Egyptians and the Nubians fought each other at some points in their history, they also respected and admired each other at other points.

Cat goddess of music

The Nubians loved cats. One ancient story told how the goddess Bastet took the form of a lioness and ran away to Nubia because she was angry with the Egyptian god Ra. The Egyptians wanted the goddess to return, so they sent the god Thoth (in the form of a monkey) to persuade her. Eventually, Bastet did return, both to the less frightening form of a pet cat and to Egypt. When she came back, she brought with her a whole gang of musicians and dancers from Nubia who followed behind her – and who brought Nubian music to Egypt.

This kind of jar was used to store the body's organs after it had been mummified. The woman whose organs it contained is sculpted into the top of the jar. She is wearing a Nubian wig.

A fine feast

The Nubians ate a huge variety of foods. We know this because of the pots for holding different foods that were found in Nubian tombs. Ceramic pots of all shapes and sizes have been found in ancient Nubia. Many of them are also beautifully decorated, which shows us that lavish dinners and parties are likely to have been an important part of life (especially for the richest Nubians).

Nubian fashion

The Nubians were famous across the ancient world for their sense of style. They wore lots of very intricate jewellery made in gold and bronze and brightly coloured clothes. Both the men and the women wore their hair in ways that other ancient people admired. In Egypt, Egyptian women of high status often wore wigs in the style of the tight curls and braids of Nubian women. The Egyptian Queen Nefertiti was the first to wear a Nubian wig – and seeing that the Queen wore a Nubian wig made other Egyptians want to do so too.

BEASTS OF THE NILE

The Nile was the key to all of life for those who lived around it. Every year the Nile would flood, leaving a fertile mud on its banks that made it possible for people to grow food to eat. But the river could also be frightening – it was full of beasts that were dangerous and powerful, like crocodiles and hippos. And sometimes an animal could look like an ordinary creature but turn out to be a goddess or a monster!

This scarab carrying the Sun was found in the tomb of King Tutankhamun. The beetle is made of precious blue lapis lazuli outlined in gold, and carries a Sun made from a carnelian stone.

Taweret the hippo goddess

Meeting a hippopotamus on the banks of the Nile would have been a terrifying experience. For the ancient Egyptians, the hippopotamus symbolised power and danger – and they were known to be able to kill people and destroy boats. But because it was the flooding of the Nile that made life possible in this region, hippopotamuses also symbolised new life and growth. The most popular god or goddess with a hippo form was Taweret. She was the goddess of childbirth and fertility and is usually shown in art with the head of a hippo, a pregnant belly, and the tail of a crocodile.

Scaly creatures

Ancient Egyptian artists had two favourite animals, the scarab beetle and the crocodile. The scarab, or dung beetle, rolls a ball of poo to eat. The ancient Egyptians thought it looked like the Sun god Ra being pushed through the sky. Thousands of scarab beetle amulets were bought by beetle fans. Tombs were often decorated with crocodiles as a sign of respect. The Egyptians feared these huge, snapping reptiles and wrote down magic spells to protect people from them. The king of the crocodiles was the powerful god Sobek, who was worshipped at a temple containing a live crocodile.

Predator praise

The Nile was also home to furry but fierce hunters such as the otter and the mongoose. Ancient Egyptian artists often showed these animals worshipping kings and gods, but sometimes it was the other way round! Otters were the special companions of the goddess Wadjet, whose job it was to protect the kings and queens of Egypt, while mongooses were considered powerful because they killed deadly snakes.

Happy hippo

This little model hippo, made in ancient Egypt, is decorated with lotus plants. These plants grow by the banks of the Nile, the hippo's natural habitat. Lotus flowers symbolise the ability to come back to life, because they close at night then open when the Sun comes up. The Egyptians believed that statues of living things could come to life, so some hippo statues had their legs broken just in case they came to life and caused chaos!

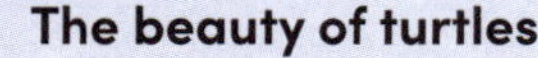

The beauty of turtles

This figurine is a tiny model of an African soft-shelled turtle. It is only about four centimetres (1.5 inches) long and is made out of semi-precious amethyst, with more valuable stones set into the back to imitate the shiny surface of a turtle's shell. Amethyst is a very difficult stone to carve so this object must have been made by a skilled artist. It was probably a very expensive object that belonged to someone rich.

TIYANAK STEALS A BABY

Strange things happened in the forest that surrounded the village where Mabute and his family lived. People would go into the trees and vanish. Or they would come out so frightened they could not even speak. Mabute had grown up being told that he should never enter the forest, and he had never questioned this wisdom. But one night something happened that made it very difficult for him to do as he was told.

Mabute was going home after playing with his friends and was just starting to think about dinner. As he walked past the dark edge of the forest he sped up, and kept his eyes firmly focused ahead of him. And that was when he heard it – the cry of a baby coming from deep within the forest. The sound stopped him in his tracks. He waited to see whether anyone would come to get their child, but no one came. The Sun was starting to set and still the baby cried and cried. Mabute knew he should not enter the forest. But surely his mother and his grandmother and everyone else in the village would understand why he had to take the risk.

Mabute took a deep breath and went into the trees, making sure that he did not fall into any traps. He made his way towards the little baby, following the sound of crying. The trees were so close together that it was pitch black – when he held his hand up, he could not even see it in front of him.

The cries got louder and louder. Eventually, he arrived in a clearing right in the middle of the forest. The baby was lying on a huge leaf on one of the lowest branches of a banana tree. It was so small that the leaf did not even droop under its weight. He reached up and lifted the baby towards him. The child was so cold. It must have been all alone in the forest for a long time.

Mabute tucked the baby inside his tunic and set off. The trees seemed to be standing even closer together now, silently watching. He started to run, jumping over branches and brushing aside vines. He looked down at the baby, who had stopped crying and started smiling. Nothing leapt out at them from the shadows. Maybe this forest wasn't so dangerous after all?

Mabute had nearly reached the edge of the forest when he began to feel something scratching at his chest. It felt as if some animal with long claws was tearing at him from underneath his tunic. He stopped running and shifted the baby – who was still smiling up at him – and carried on. But the scratching did not stop. Mabute thought it was very strange that a baby could have such long, sharp nails. Suddenly Mabute cried out in pain – "OW!" he shouted. The baby had sunk its teeth into the fleshy part of his arm. This did not make sense at all – tiny little babies do not have sharp teeth!

He lifted the child back out and held it up when all of a sudden it started to change shape. Its legs and arms grew until they were almost the length of an adult's, and a long beard sprouted from its chin. Wings with black feathers popped out from its shoulders, and it grew hundreds of years older in only a few moments. Mabute stared in horror – he knew what this creature was: not a baby, but a Tiyanak. He dropped the fierce creature and ran for his life. He did not stop until he was out of the forest and all the way home. He glanced back just once, and saw the Tiyanak flapping its dark wings and flying away into the forest.

Mabute's mother was waiting for him when he got home. His aunt was there, who lived on the other side of the village, and Mabute could see that she had been crying. His mother asked him to explain where he had been – it had been dark for hours, and she had been worrying about him. But when he explained that he had gone into the forest because he had heard a baby crying, his mother and his aunt were not angry. They looked happier than he had ever seen them look. Earlier that day, his aunt explained, a Tiyanak had come and stolen away her newborn baby. Everyone in the village had been out searching everywhere – except, of course, the forest, where they all knew it was far too dangerous to go. She had tears in her eyes as she hugged Mabute close and thanked him for rescuing her baby – but where was the child?

As gently as he could, Mabute told them everything that had happened, including how the baby had transformed itself into a Tiyanak and flown away. His own mother was so grateful that her son was safe and had returned from the forest alive. But the three of them cried together for his aunt, whose baby had been stolen away by the Tiyanak.

THE PONATURI KIDNAP TĀWHAKI'S FAMILY

Tāwhaki and his younger brother Karihi lived in a home surrounded by high walls, at the very top of the tallest mountain. They felt safe here, protected from the dangerous beasts that threatened people outside. But walls rarely make those inside as safe as they feel. One day fierce beasts, thousands of them, snuck in through the cracks in the walls and stole Tāwhaki and Karihi's father and grandmother away.

It was the Ponaturi who had done this, tiny creatures that walked upright like humans but also flew through the air on silent wings. During the day they lived at the very bottom of the sea. But at night they made their way out of the water to sleep in a house that many thousands of them shared together. There was no one who was not afraid of them. In a house down by the shore there lived a man called Ruapupuke, whose son had been taken by the Ponaturi. Ruapupuke had dived all the way down to the bottom of the sea, but when he arrived his son was nowhere to be seen. The Ponaturi had killed him, and carved flutes and drums out of his bones.

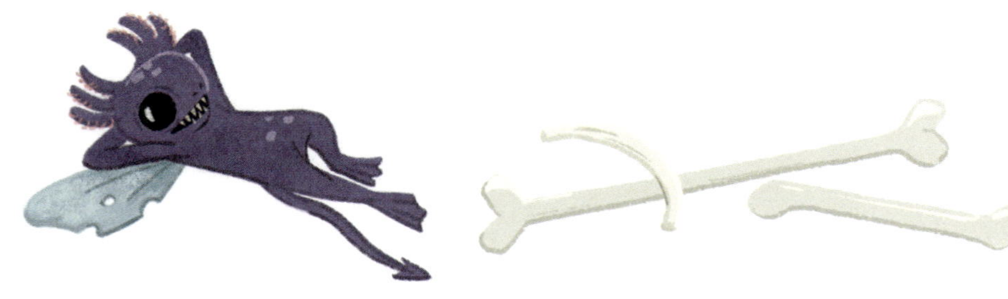

Tāwhaki and Karihi were afraid of what the tiny monsters might do to their father and grandmother. The Sun was about to set, so they ran to the house where the Ponaturi slept at night-time. They hid behind a small bush by the front door and waited for night to come. As soon as it was dark, thousands of tiny beasts flocked to the house and squeezed through the gaps around the edges of the door. The Ponaturi did not struggle to see their way. They lived their whole lives in darkness, so their eyes were used to it. Tāwhaki and Karihi were not used to seeing in the dark, but from the light of the fire inside the house, they could make out the shape of their grandmother, Whaitiri, standing in the doorway. She was handing out small baskets of food to each of the Ponaturi one by one. Whaitiri was completely blind, and so the darkness did not stop her from carrying out her task.

For a moment Tāwhaki and Karihi stood in silence. It was such a surprise to see their grandmother, who was usually so powerful and strong, quietly handing out food to the Ponaturi who had kidnapped her. As well as being their grandmother, Whaitiri was also the goddess of thunder. Tāwhaki thought that he could hear the sky rumbling quietly above them, letting them know that she was not happy.

Once the Ponaturi had all gone into the house and fallen asleep, Tāwhaki and Karihi whispered to Whaitiri. They asked her two questions: what had happened – and where their father was. This second question made Whaitiri start to cry, and the thunder that had been quietly rumbling in the night sky suddenly crashed loudly. There were three bright flashes of lightning that showed the brothers how upset Whaitiri was.

The boys' grandmother gestured for them to look around the room. The boys saw carvings made of bone hanging on each of the walls. There were almost as many carvings as there are bones in the human body. It was then that they realised that they had not made it in time to save their father. The Ponaturi had killed him, just like they had killed the son of Ruapupuke. And they had turned his bones into carved instruments. But there was no time for them to let their sadness and grief take over. If they did not get out of here before the Ponaturi woke up, their own bones and their grandmother's would be turned into carved instruments too.

Maori flutes, 19th century

These flutes are made from wood rather than human bones. But if you look closely you can see they are carved with monstrous faces, that would have looked at home in the house of the Ponaturi.

Whaitiri had lived much longer than Tāwhaki or Karihi and so she knew much more than they did about the Ponaturi. "The only thing that will kill them," she said, "is sunlight. But where will we find the Sun in the middle of the night?" Karihi had an idea. Each morning, the Ponaturi returned to the sea when the Sun rose. If they could not tell that the Sun was rising, then they would not start their journey back to the sea. They waited for the Ponaturi to go to sleep, then he told Tāwhaki and Whaitiri to gather as many leaves as they could from the trees nearby and use them to block up all of the windows in the house. Once every window was covered, they waited.

Karihi's plan worked. The Sun began to rise, but the Ponaturi slept soundly in the darkness inside of the house, completely unaware of what had happened. When the Sun had risen to its highest point, Whaitiri and the two brothers removed the leaves from the windows and the Sun streamed through the house. The moment the sunlight touched the Ponaturi, they vanished instantly – and they were never able to carve up anyone else's family again.

IFE AND THE DEEP WATER

In every house in every village, mothers told their children not to swim too far out into the water. Their own mothers had told them the same story. In the deep waters there was a creature so powerful that no one dared to come near to her. The people in Ife's home town called her Mami Wata. She had the body of a woman with the tail of a dolphin and carried a snake wrapped around her neck and shoulders.

No one knew whether Mami Wata used her powers for good or bad. Generations of people decided it would be better never to find out. There were some who found Mami Wata difficult to avoid, though. The fishermen and fisherwomen had to take their boats out to the deep water, where the fish were bigger. Occasionally one of the fishers would go missing, and people would say that Mami Wata had taken them down to the deepest depths. Only one person who went missing ever came back.

Ife made her living rowing her little boat out onto the river, catching fish to sell in the village. Every day she caught

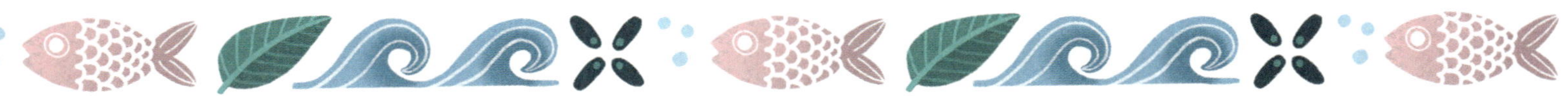

enough fish to feed her own family and a little extra that she could sell, but never more. Every day she had to get back into her boat and go out fishing again. Ife knew that going out to the deepest part of the river was dangerous. She had heard the stories about Mami Wata, the woman with a dolphin's tail, who lived there. But every day she was tempted to row her boat a little further out, to catch bigger fish to feed her family.

One day Ife rowed out too far. The water was dark and deep here and although she could see plenty of huge fish swimming close to the surface, she could no longer see the bottom. It was then that she heard a strange sound – like someone was singing, only Ife could not see anyone else around. The sound was a low note that seemed to be coming from the water. And as the sound got louder and louder Ife realised that it was not a song, but a hiss. She picked up her oars and tried to row back to where the water was not so dark and deep. But before she had managed to move even an inch, an enormous creature burst out of the water.

Mami Wata

There are many myths about water because it is vital to our survival but also has power that can be scary. The water spirit Mami Wata is celebrated in West Africa and the Caribbean for bringing wealth. She is shown here with a gigantic snake wrapped around her.

Ife recognised her instantly. Where the woman's legs might be, she had the tail of a pink dolphin. There was seaweed in her curly black hair and an enormous snake wrapped around her neck (which was hissing angrily). It was Mami Wata. Ife opened her mouth to explain she had not meant any harm. She had only wanted to catch some of the bigger fish for her family to eat. But Mami Wata kicked her tail, sending a wave that overturned Ife's little boat. Ife tried to swim to the shore but Mami Wata grabbed her in one huge hand and held her up to her face so that she could get a better look at her.

"There is no shame," Mami Wata said in a soft voice, "in wanting to feed your family." Then she kicked her fins and flew up into the air before diving deep into the water, with Ife still in a tight grip. They swam down and down into the darkest depths. Just as Ife thought that she would run out of breath, they burst through the sandy bottom of the riverbed. Ife suddenly found she could breathe as if she was on land. This place was unlike anywhere she had been before – in fact, it was unlike anything she could even have dreamed of. Her worst fear had always been that she would not be able to catch enough fish to feed her family. In this place, she couldn't imagine anyone ever worrying about that. Everywhere she looked were enormous platters filled with delicious things to eat. Vines hung from above,

each one heavy with fresh fruit. Ife sat down and ate until she was full, but no matter how much she ate the plate in front of her was still full of food.

When she was finished, Mami Wata pulled out a bag full of gold and jewels and gave it to Ife. "Take this," she said, "and you will never need to fish for food for your family again." And with that she snatched Ife up in her fist once again, kicked with her fins and took her back up through the water to the land. She put Ife down on the shore, and before she swam back off to the deepest depths she smiled and said, "Tell everyone who lives in the village that there is no need to be afraid of Mami Wata. Tell them that Mami Wata would give them everything they ever dreamed of if only they rowed out to the depths." And when Ife got home, she told the other humans exactly that – but none of them believed her.

BATTLES WITH MONSTERS

At the heart of many of the stories we tell about beasts and monsters is a simple question: will good be able to defeat evil? The stakes are high. When humans fight with beasts they risk losing everything – not just their own lives but the entire world as they know it. And humans know that when they battle with monsters the chances of them winning are not good. The beasts in these stories are usually bigger, stronger, and fiercer than humans are. But the humans go into battle anyway, because of what they stand to lose if they don't. Good might not always defeat evil but humans will go to great lengths to try and make sure it does.

DURGA FIGHTS THE BUFFALO DEMON

All across the land, everyone knew the name of the buffalo demon. They knew because people screamed, "Look out, it's Mahishasura!" while running away from the demon, who had been terrorising them for as long as they could remember. Mahishasura seemed to hate everything good in the world. And no one could stop this terrible beast because the God Brahma had made it impossible for him to die – or at least so everyone thought.

Most of the time Mahishasura appeared in the form of a huge buffalo with sharp horns and even sharper teeth. He was so full of anger and violence that there was almost no room in him for any good – but in the eyes of the gods he did have one good quality. He never forgot to worship the God Brahma. After many years of prayers and offerings, Brahma decided to reward him.

Mahishasura knew immediately what to ask for. He asked Brahma to make it so that he could never die. But Brahma told him it was simply a fact of life that everyone must one day die. Mahishasura thought about this for a moment and then said, "In that case, make it so that no man, god, demon, or beast will be able to kill me!" Mahishasura laughed to himself. In his mind, this was the same as asking for immortality. It didn't occur to him to include women in his wish.

Brahma granted his wish, and Mahishasura returned to terrorising the humans. Next, Mahishasura made a terrible mistake. He began attacking gods as well as humans. This was the last straw. The gods went to the three most powerful Gods, Brahma, Shiva, and Vishnu, and asked for help. Brahma, Shiva, and Vishnu knew they couldn't defeat Mahishasura themselves because of his wish. Instead they created a super-strong woman called Durga. They, and the other gods, made copies of their weapons, including a trident and a bow and arrow. They handed the weapons to Durga and told her they had a task for her. They wanted her to defeat the buffalo demon once and for all. Durga smiled, because it sounded to her like light work.

Divine buffalo

Although Mahishasura the buffalo demon is destructive, Indian art often celebrates the animal, a type of wild cattle. Here the god Yama rides a beautifully decorated buffalo.

Durga did not waste a moment before getting started on her task. Instead of walking, she jumped onto the back of a lion created just for her. Carrying each of her weapons, she set off in search of the buffalo demon. Mahishasura was not difficult to find, because he was making a loud roaring sound and destroying a village with his enormous horns. Durga called out to him, and he turned around to look at her, riding on a huge lion with her hands full of weapons. The buffalo demon was astonished.

As impressive as Durga was, Mahishasura did not even try to run away, because he was so sure that there could never be a woman strong enough to kill him. He started to laugh at the idea that a woman might ever defeat him. But before it could even reach the ears of the frightened villagers, his mocking laughter was silenced. Durga came towards him wielding a weapon in each hand. After a long, difficult fight, Mahishasura lay dead at her feet.

The gods were delighted and the humans clapped and cheered with relief. They thanked Brahma, Shiva, and Vishnu for saving them from this monster. Most of all they thanked Durga for her bravery in going into battle to protect them. The demon was gone once and for all. Durga was still smiling. She knew that no one would ever again think that women were not strong enough to do anything they set their minds to.

RA AND SET VERSUS THE ENEMY OF LIGHT

Ra and Apep came into the world at almost the same moment. After Ra was born, Apep came to life from the cord that was still connecting baby Ra to his mother. But Ra and Apep could not have been more different. Ra was the god of light, responsible for steering a ship with the Sun in it across the sky every day. Apep was an enormous serpent. He hated light and wanted the whole world to be in darkness.

Ra and his boat were always moving. By day they carried the Sun and its light across the sky. By night they sailed through the darkness of the underworld. It was here that he encountered Apep. The giant serpent hissed and spat at Ra and chased him through the underworld, snapping his jaws. But although Apep's teeth were frightening enough, there was something else about him that was much more dangerous. Apep's glowing eyes could petrify anyone he looked at so that they froze and could not move. Anyone, that is, except Set the god of storms. So Ra always took Set with him into the underworld to protect him from the serpent. But one day the Sun came close to never rising again.

That night was much like any other. As Ra and Set moved through the underworld, Apep appeared. Ra was petrified, but as Apep snapped his jaws at the boat, Set did his best to steer the boat to safety. Tonight though, Set's best was not good enough. Apep snapped his jaws shut on the back of the ship – with the Sun balanced between his fangs. Set tried everything he could but the boat would not move. He began to imagine what the world would be like if it was forever in darkness. He could not allow that to happen.

Quietly, so that Apep would not hear, Set began to recite the words of a spell. He had used this spell before, which is how he knew that its magic could bind up his enemy and tie them in place – but he had never used it on a beast as huge or as fierce as Apep. He spoke the words over and over.

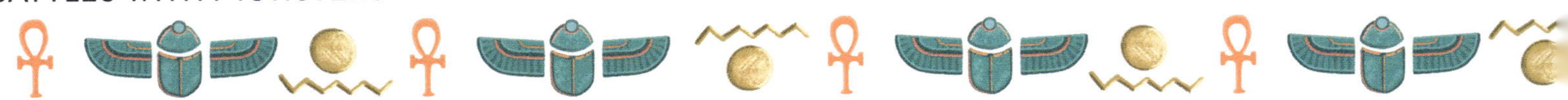

Suddenly Set felt Apep's grip on the boat relax. The spell was working. The boat dropped back out of the serpent's jaws and into the water. Apep writhed and roared, unable to understand what it was that was holding him back. Set took out his sword and cut the snake's body into pieces, thinking that this would make it impossible for Apep to ever threaten the world with darkness ever again. Then he steered the boat away as quickly as he could, and he did not stop until the Sun was beginning to rise and Ra was waking up from the trance Apep had put him in.

Set was wrong to think that he had defeated Apep forever. By some kind of magic that neither the gods nor the humans understood, Apep was back the next night. Every night Apep petrified Ra with his gleaming eyes, and every night Set had to cast his spell and kill the giant serpent over and over again. Every night the whole world was almost thrown into darkness forever, but every morning the Sun rose over the horizon again.

Tomb decoration
13th century BCE

The Egyptian pharoah Seti I died in 1279 BCE, and his tomb was richly decorated. This painting shows the god Ra sailing through the underworld, surrounded by the coils of a snake.

If you had asked the humans – rather than the gods – what it was that was most frightening about Apep, they would have said that it was his ear-splitting roar. When Apep roared, the Earth shook and the sky cracked open with thunder. While they were in the land of the living, this sound was all the humans ever knew of Apep. They were worried about what awaited them when they met Apep in the underworld. Set gave them a special spell to protect them, like the one he used every night (but one that would work for humans and not just for gods). He told them to craft an image of Apep for their tombs. This, he said, would protect them from the monster. And so when the humans buried their loved ones, they always made sure that they had an image of Apep with them, to protect them from the terrifying serpent.

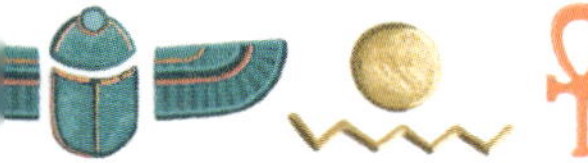

DANGEROUS DRAGONS AND SLITHERING SNAKES

Because a snake's whole body touches the ground as it moves, many ancient people thought that they had a role to play in the natural cycles of the Earth. Others thought that shedding their skins made them immortal. These magic properties may be why many stories about how the world began started with a snake. From real snakes rose the legend of the dragon, a huge version of the reptiles found all over the world.

Although in real life snakes can be dangerous, the ancient Egyptians used snakes as a symbol of protection. Women carried amulets like this one with them to gain Hathor's protection.

Snake gods and goddesses

Many ancient Egyptian gods and goddesses could take the form of a snake. The goddess Hathor was usually shown as a cobra with a human head. Hathor was a protector of women, and other snake gods were also viewed in a positive light. In Egyptian mythology, one of the first gods to come into existence was the snake god Nehebkau. He was one of the judges of whether human souls had been good or bad, which gave him immense power, but the Egyptians thought of him as a kindly god rather than just a judgemental one.

Cypriot snakes

On the island of Cyprus, snakes were thought to be symbols of fertility and new life by the ancient people who lived there. Cypriot artists started making pictures of their slithery neighbours as far back as 7,000 years ago! This limestone sculpture shows a snake-charmer holding a snake in each hand and with the bodies of three more snakes on his head. Snake-charmers could supposedly cure snake bites by touching the victim or sucking at the wound – they were called Ophiogeneis, which means 'Snakeborn'.

Chinese dragon

Unlike European dragons, Chinese dragons do not breathe fire. In fact, they are usually in charge of water and rainfall – and for this reason they are very important. Ancient China was a place that depended on watering and growing crops, and so the dragon was seen as a mostly well-meaning spirit living in the sky. The emperors of China had a special relationship with the dragon, and were the only ones allowed to wear dragon images on their robes. Images of dragons were also often used to decorate the tombs and houses of powerful people, and worn as jewellery.

Marduk's pet dragon

Marduk was the king of the ancient Mesopotamian gods and also the god in charge of protecting the city of Babylon (in what is now Iraq). Marduk and his son Nabu kept a dragon as their pet. The dragon helped to protect them and their city – like a guard dog. The gates of the city were decorated with images of this dragon and other frightening animals, to scare away anyone who might try to enter the city and harm its inhabitants. The dragon was also carved into objects found in temples and other important buildings in the city.

The Antaboga

Many ancient stories about the creation of the world began with a snake or dragon. For the ancient Javanese people of Indonesia, the world began with a dragon called Antaboga.
The dragon meditated quietly before time began and created Bedawang, the giant turtle who carried the world on her back. On Bedawang's back there was also a black stone, which was the door between the human world and the underworld. Without Antaboga, nothing in the world could exist.

THE TWINS SAVE THE WORLD FROM YEITSO

Nayenezgani and Tobadzischini were the twin sons of Changing Woman, who had turned her own skin into all of the humans who lived in the world. Their father was the Sun itself. But despite their powerful parents, for as long as they could remember, they had been afraid of Yeitso. Yeitso was a giant so huge he could cover the whole of the Earth in three steps. He could drink the ocean in two gulps. And his voice was so loud that even his whisper made the ground shake. Yeitso hated the twins because their father was the Sun and he wanted the whole world to be in darkness.

When he found out where Changing Woman lived, Yeitso took one big step from the other side of the world to her house. She hid the children under her cloak and said, "You are mistaken, Yeitso. There are no children here." Yeitso looked at the ground in front of the house, which was covered in snow. "If there are no children here," he asked, "then whose are these footprints?" Changing Woman had to think quickly. "I am so lonely," she said,

"I made the footprints myself, so I could pretend I had a friend." Yeitso thought about this carefully. He had heard that loneliness was something humans felt. He did not know that goddesses like Changing Woman could suffer with it too. But it seemed a likely explanation. He left – but not for long.

Each time Yeitso returned, Changing Woman managed to fool him. But as the boys got older, they decided to put an end to the monster. They needed help, so they went to find Spider Grandmother, who was older than time itself and lived in a hole she had dug back when the world was new. She taught the humans how to weave cloth from wool in order to keep themselves warm. And she knew how to defeat a giant.

Spider Grandmother was not the kind of creature who needed to be told about a problem twice before she came up with a plan to solve it. "Take these feathers," she said to the twins. "Use them like shields to protect you." Tobadzischini was not sure how a feather would protect them from being attacked by a monster, but Nayenezgani told him to trust Spider Grandmother. Then she told them to go and visit their father, the god of the Sun.

Before they left Spider Grandmother's home, Nayenezgani asked, "How will we climb all the way up to the highest point of the sky where our father lives?" Spider Grandmother took a piece of the silver thread that lined the walls of her home, and threw it towards the sky. Nayenezgani and Tobadzischini watched as it flew higher and higher. Eventually, it wrapped itself around the edge of a cloud. "Pull!" she shouted, and the twins grabbed onto the silver thread and pulled. When they had pulled the cloud low enough to the ground, the twins jumped up onto it.

They climbed into the sky in this way, hopping from one cloud to the next as they floated up. But even people who arrived on the clouds were not allowed to just walk into this palace in the sky. A whole army of guards were standing in front of the gates. They looked intimidating and had long spears. The twins racked their brains. Eventually, Tobadzischini shrugged. Their mother had always told them that nothing was stronger than the truth. He walked forward and told the guards that they had spent their

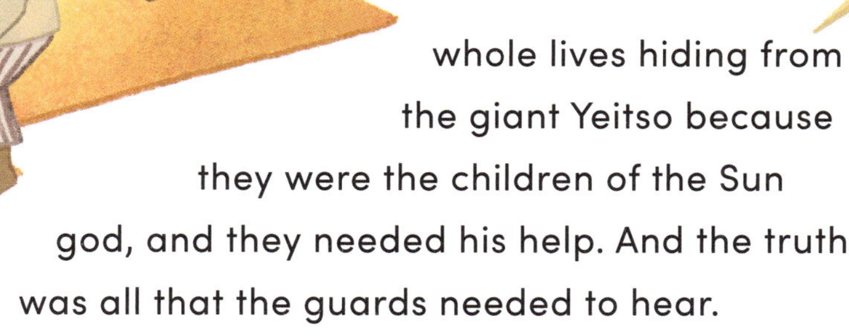

whole lives hiding from the giant Yeitso because they were the children of the Sun god, and they needed his help. And the truth was all that the guards needed to hear.

Their father was so pleased to see his sons that he offered them anything they could see from up there in the sky as a gift. "We haven't come for any of those things, father," said Tobadzischini. Nayenezgani continued, "All we need is the lightning bolts that you keep up here in your palace, so that we can defeat Yeitso." The Sun god fetched the lightning bolts immediately. Then he brought an even larger lightning bolt and told the twins to climb onto it. He threw the lightning bolt back down to the Earth with the boys riding on top, and it landed in the pool of water where Yeitso came once a day to drink. The boys hid nearby and waited.

The twins hit Yeitso with a lightning bolt as soon as he opened his mouth to gulp down all of the water in the pool. Neither the twins, nor their mother, were ever bothered by Yeitso again. And the world never did descend into total darkness.

Sun kachina
20th century
The indigenous Hopi people of southwest North America tell stories about spirits called kachinas. They make dolls, also called kachinas, to represent the spirits, such as this one made to represent the Sun spirit Tawa.

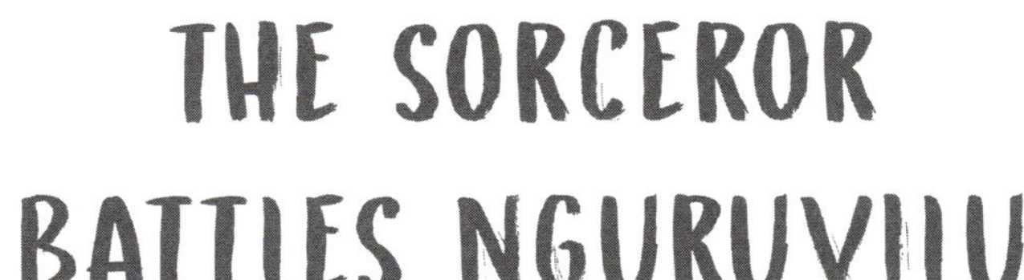

THE SORCEROR BATTLES NGURUVILU

Once, there were two villages that stood on either side of a river. Usually the river kept its waters low so that the villagers could cross from one village to the other simply by wading in up to their knees. The villagers fed themselves with fish from the river and wove baskets from its reeds. They respected the river, which in turn respected them. But one day, everything changed.

It was a young man named Malku who noticed it first. Malku sat every day by the banks of the river weaving baskets. He was in love with a young man who lived in the next village and he often crossed the river to see him. But today was not like all the other days he had made the crossing. As he stepped into the river he noticed that the water rose up almost to his chest.

The river was not flowing in its usual direction. Instead of gently moving downstream, as it had done for as long as Malku could remember, the river was turning in a circle. The circle was getting bigger and bigger, and the river was flowing faster and faster. White froth appeared at the top of the water and the sound was so loud that Malku had to cover his ears and step back from the edge of the river. "HELP!" he shouted. "Something terrible has happened to the river!"

On both sides of the river, people came out of their houses to see what was happening. Some of them came as fast as they could, while the elders followed more slowly. An old woman approached Malku. She had an idea about what had happened because she had seen it before, back when she was just a little girl. The old woman said, "It was Nguruvilu who is to blame."

Malku had never heard of Nguruvilu. The old woman told him that he was a monster that looked a bit like a fox. He had a body that was stretched out like a snake's, with a long tail. He could use his tail, the old woman explained, to beat the riverbed and cause enormous whirlpools. No human had ever attempted to cross one of Nguruvilu's whirlpools and survived. But she had an idea. "Fetch the Machi," the old woman said, "she is the only one who can help us." She remembered that when she was just a little girl, the Machi had saved the village then too. Malku ran in the direction of the Machi's house as fast as he could.

The Machi was a sorcerer, wise beyond her years. And most importantly, she was a very strong swimmer. Only a Machi would dare to swim anywhere near Nguruvilu. When Malku returned with the Machi, the whirlpool was even bigger, swirling faster and faster. Without saying a word, the sorcerer tied back her long hair with a length of wool and plunged into the water. The whirlpool kept swirling, and the villagers could not see what was happening. A long time passed – much longer than any human could have held their breath for. And still the Machi did not surface.

Underwater, a battle was raging. The Machi used strength, determination, and magical powers to swim against the flow of water to the bottom of the river. Eventually, she came face to face with Nguruvilu. He was spinning in a furious circle, venting all his anger and frustration. The Machi swum towards the monster in one powerful movement and wrestled him to the ground. He fought fiercely until eventually he realised that she was stronger than he was. The fight went out of Nguruvilu and he stopped spinning. Then, holding Nguruvilu in her arms like he was a sweet little puppy and not a fierce river monster, the Machi returned to the surface.

With all of the villagers from both villages watching, the Machi told Nguruvilu, "Do not return to this river ever again, unless you want to find out how powerful I really am!" she said. Nguruvilu did not want to find out what else the Machi could do. With his tail between his legs, the monster slid back into the river and swam away downstream – and was never seen by the villagers again.

The whirlpool slowed down, and eventually stopped swirling altogether, and the river was calm again. The villagers clapped and cheered, and thanked the Machi for making the river calm again. And Malku waded across to be reunited with the man he loved.

HALF-HUMAN BEASTS

Many beasts from the ancient world remind us of ourselves. Ancient people often imagined monsters who were half-human and half something else, like a god or an animal. These special creatures were sometimes part of families where one parent was a human and the other was not. But they could also be born by other, more magical means. However they came about in ancient cultures, they were always a sign of ancient people asking big questions about the place of humans in the world.

Man or bull?

The queen of Crete fell in love with a bull and gave birth to a child who was half-man, half-bull, called the Minotaur. As he grew up, the creature began to eat human beings, so he was locked up in a labyrinth from which he could not escape. Every year seven boys and seven girls from Athens were sent to Crete to be fed to the Minotaur as a sacrifice – until the hero Theseus decided to put an end to this. With the help of a princess called Ariadne, he killed the Minotaur. Theseus escaped, and Athenian families never lost their children to the monster again. This Greek vase from around 500 BCE shows Theseus killing the Minotaur.

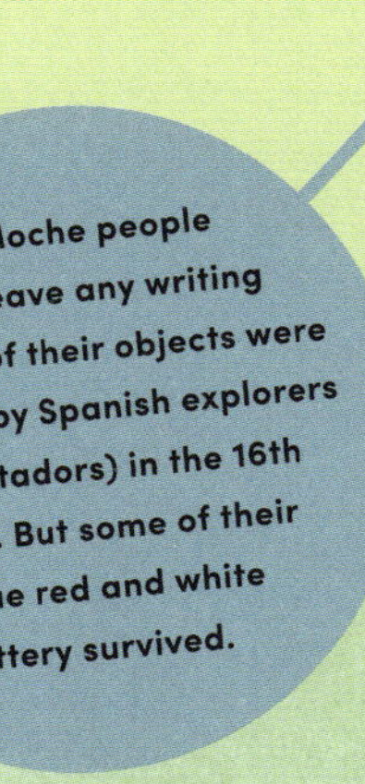

The Moche people didn't leave any writing and many of their objects were destroyed by Spanish explorers (conquistadors) in the 16th century. But some of their unique red and white pottery survived.

Handy birds

The ancient Moche people lived on the North coast of Peru from around 100–700 CE. Farming was very important to their way of life, and they also were very skilled artists. They were especially good at making pottery and ceramics, and used moulds which allowed them to make pottery in very complicated shapes. Many of these ceramic vessels were in shapes of half-human, half-animal creatures – especially birds. This ceramic vessel has the body of a bird but human hands.

Kinnara

The Kinnaras were half-human and half-bird. They were known for falling in love once and never changing their mind or loving anyone else. They never had any offspring, and instead lived happily with their partners up in the mountains. They also made music so beautiful that all the gods and goddesses asked them to be their own musicians. These creatures are seen in pictures and sculptures all across Southeast Asia.

Centaur

In Greek mythology, the centaur is a beast with the upper body and head of a human (usually a man) and the lower body and legs of a horse. The wisest of all the centaurs was called Chiron. The god Apollo had taught him everything he knew about music, art, and medicine. Many of the heroes of Greek myth were sent to learn from him, including Hercules. Other groups of ancient people also spoke of similar half-man, half-horse creatures – like Tumburu in Hindu mythology and the Polkan of early Russian tales.

Half-human puppies

The Inuit people of Greenland tell stories about a mythical creature called the Adlet. An Adlet has the lower body of a dog and the upper body of a human.
The story goes that they were born when a woman called Niviarsiang refused to marry any human man. Eventually, she married a dog called Ijirqang instead. Together Niviarsiang and Ijirqang had ten children. Five of the children were ordinary dogs, and the other five were Adlet.

Human or creature?

The art of ancient Iran is full of magical creatures who are half-human and half-animal. This silver statue shows a bull behaving like a human, lifting a vessel. We do not know what role the people of ancient Iran believed these human-like animals played. But we do know that these creatures were an important part of the world they inhabited.
This creature may have appeared in a popular story we no longer remember. Imagine if it was the main character in your favourite TV show!

BELLEROPHON AND PEGASUS FIGHT THE CHIMERA

Bellerophon was unlucky in love. It wasn't that he loved a person who did not love him back, but that he did not love someone who did. Stheneboea was her name, the daughter of King Iobates of Lykia. When Bellerophon told her that he did not love her back, at least not the way that she loved him, Stheneboea asked her father to punish him. The spiteful king was all too quick to agree. He gave Bellerophon the worst punishment he could think of: to kill the fierce Chimera.

Bellerophon had no choice but to obey, but he was frightened. The Chimera was not one monster, but three monsters in one. She had the body of a lion, the tail of a dragon, and the head of a goat, with huge horns sticking out of her back. And what made her more frightening than all of this, was the fact that she could breathe fire. As Bellerophon was collecting his weapons together and preparing to leave the city, the king came to find him. He taunted him, saying, "So you think, Bellerophon, that you don't need a partner like my daughter because you can manage all on your own? Let's see how you do against the Chimera – alone." The king smiled to himself, because he knew that the Chimera was more than a match for a single person, even a hero. But Bellerophon wasn't on his own.

He had a winged horse called Pegasus who never left his side. Bellerophon jumped onto the back of his trusty friend, and they rode out of the city. The king called after them, in front of all of his citizens: "I'd bet my whole kingdom," he said – and now he was laughing out loud – "that you can't kill this monster!" Neither Bellerophon nor Pegasus answered.

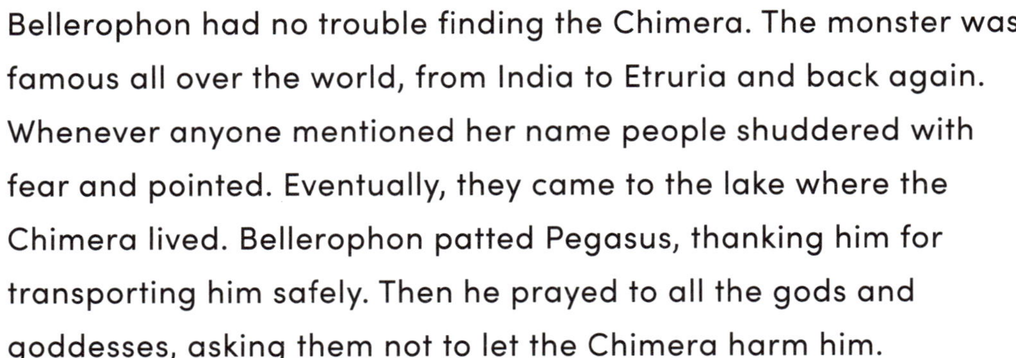

Bellerophon had no trouble finding the Chimera. The monster was famous all over the world, from India to Etruria and back again. Whenever anyone mentioned her name people shuddered with fear and pointed. Eventually, they came to the lake where the Chimera lived. Bellerophon patted Pegasus, thanking him for transporting him safely. Then he prayed to all the gods and goddesses, asking them not to let the Chimera harm him.

Bellerophon prayed as quietly as he could, but not quietly enough. The Chimera heard the sound of his voice and woke up. Her eyes landed on Bellerophon. He and Pegasus tried to run but it was too late. The Chimera was much faster than a horse, even a horse as strong as Pegasus. "Run, Pegasus!" Bellerophon shouted, sliding down off the horse's back. "Save your own life! It's me who the king ordered to fight the monster, not you!" But Pegasus refused to move. He could not leave his friend all alone.

Instead, he grabbed the fabric of Bellerophon's tunic with his teeth, and threw him onto his back. He set off as fast as he could go – not running this time, but flying. Using his enormous golden wings he could move much faster than he could run. And the Chimera, for all her power, could not fly. Bellerophon tried to call out to his friend, "Pegasus, wh-wh-what are you doing?" But Pegasus did not hear him. He kept on flying up and up and up, until they were so high in the sky that the enormous lion body of the Chimera looked like a tiny little kitten.

Bellerophon took out an arrow, and aimed very carefully. He let it fly. They were too far away to see clearly, but by the sound they heard next they could tell that Bellerophon had not missed his target. It was somewhere between the bleat of a goat and the roar of a lion – but as loud as an earthquake.

Eventually, Bellerophon and Pegasus returned to solid ground, and went back to the city that King Iobates ruled. Bellerophon told the king what he had done. He made sure to say that he had not managed it all alone – he could not have done it without his faithful friend Pegasus. And there was nothing the king could do other than hand over his whole kingdom, as he had promised.

MAGICAL HORSES

More than any other animal, horses are given magical powers in stories and myths. It is easy to understand when you think about how important horses were to ancient people around the world. Before cars or aeroplanes or buses or trains existed, horses were how people travelled and carried heavy burdens. It is not surprising that so many stories are about these fast, strong, and loyal animals.

Longma

Horses with magical powers played a very important role in Chinese mythology. The Longma had the body of a horse but also had wings and was scaly like a dragon – and it could walk on water without sinking! The Longma was said to be an important spirit of heaven and Earth, and to have been born out of the river. It also had a very important job. When a Longma appeared, people said that it was proof that a good leader had taken up the throne. Chinese emperors probably encouraged people to think they had seen the Longma!

This model of a flying horse is carved out of ivory. It was made around three thousand years ago in the area that is now Iran.

Flying horses

From the ancient Greek magical horse Pegasus to the 'lightning-fast' Buraq of Islamic writings, from the Wind Horse of ancient Tibet to the early Chinese Tianma (who could sweat blood), horses with wings have always had a special place in myth. They often had close friendships with human heroes, helping them on their quests and adventures. Although real-life horses couldn't fly, they were crucial for helping humans to travel long distances, so taking to the air was the next step in imagining what horses could do.

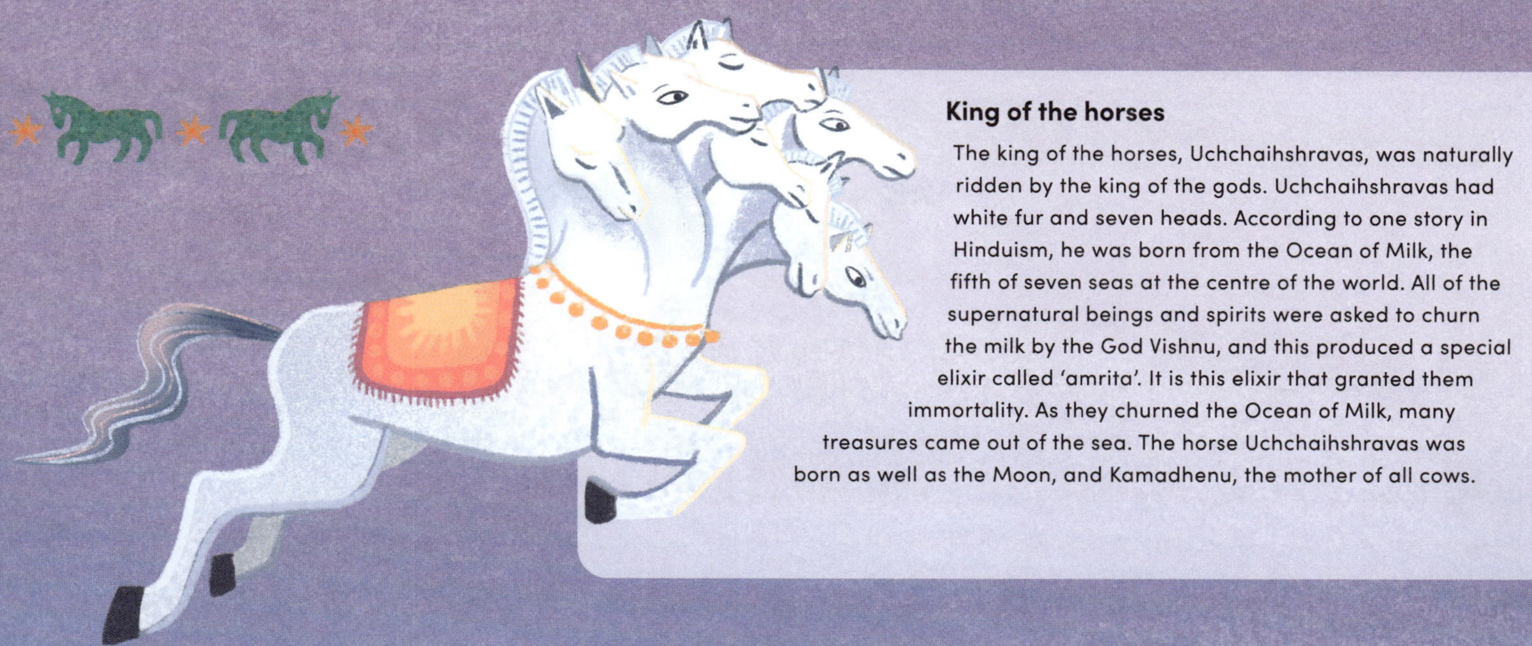

King of the horses

The king of the horses, Uchchaihshravas, was naturally ridden by the king of the gods. Uchchaihshravas had white fur and seven heads. According to one story in Hinduism, he was born from the Ocean of Milk, the fifth of seven seas at the centre of the world. All of the supernatural beings and spirits were asked to churn the milk by the God Vishnu, and this produced a special elixir called 'amrita'. It is this elixir that granted them immortality. As they churned the Ocean of Milk, many treasures came out of the sea. The horse Uchchaihshravas was born as well as the Moon, and Kamadhenu, the mother of all cows.

Chariot of the Sun

For many ancient people, mythical horses had a very important role in carrying the Sun. The ancient Baltic people, who lived in what is now Estonia, Latvia, and Lithuania, said that horses with golden fur and fiery manes and tails pulled the Sun's chariot. At night the horses swam through the sea, dragging the chariot behind them. The Greeks believed that the Sun god, Helios, drove a chariot pulled by horses. And horses pulled the Mesopotamian Sun god Utu's chariot across the sky each day too. These myths helped ancient people to explain the great mystery of how the Sun rose every morning and set every evening.

The Tikbalang

Deep in the rainforests of the ancient Philippines, there lived a terrifying creature called the Tikbalang. The creature stood on two legs, like a human, but had the head and hooves of a horse. Anyone who went into the forest had to ask permission from the Tikbalang or risk being led astray and never coming home again. In order to tame it, a brave human would have to leap onto the Tikbalang's back and then hang on tight as it flew through the sky and tried to shake off its rider. The story of the Tikbalang has been told for thousands of years, but horses are not native to the islands of the Philippines. The creature's horse shape is thought to be inspired by Hayagriva, the name given to Vishnu when he takes the form of a horse.

APUKOHAI, MONSTER OF THE DEEP

Kawelo had loved Kaakauhuhimalani, the chief of his village, for as long as he could remember. And she had finally agreed to marry him. Kawelo had spent years learning to fish, grow crops, and anything he thought might make him a good husband. But it was not until he learnt to dance the hula that the chief fell in love.

But his brothers were not as happy for Kawelo as he had expected them to be. They were annoyed that by marrying the chief he had become more powerful than them. So they told Kawelo to fetch his canoe and row away from the island of Kauai, or face the consequences. Kawelo knew they would kill him rather than lose their power over him. He danced once last sad hula with his wife and then he got into his boat and rowed away.

Kawelo was strong, and even the highest waves did not worry him. He prayed to the creator god Kane to keep him safe, and kept on rowing day after day. There was something else that did worry him, though. Kaakauhuhimalani had told him stories about a monster who lived in the deep sea called Apukohai. Kawelo watched the water nervously but saw no sign of the monster.

Eventually, Kawelo arrived at the island of O'ahu. He was welcomed by the chief and lived happily in a little house by the sea. Happily, that is, except for the fact that he missed his wife. Each morning, when the Sun rose, he stood at the edge of the waves and looked out to the horizon. He would dance a sad hula, and ask the winds to tell his wife that he missed her.

Years passed. During his time on O'ahu, Kawelo adopted a son, Kauluiki. They made a good team, this orphaned boy and the man with no family. Kauluiki grew into a young man and Kawelo decided it was time to bring his son home. They got into their boat and set off for Kauai. This time the waves seemed much calmer than they had been when Kawelo had navigated them all those years ago. It was almost like the sea wanted him to return to Kauai. But the gentle lapping of the sea hid something dangerous.

Fish hook
18th century

When brave Hawaiians like Kawelo set out on the ocean waves, it was to fish and explore. They caught fish using hooks like this one, made from wood and a gleaming substance called mother-of-pearl, which is found inside some seashells.

It was Kauluiki who noticed it first. A dark shadow underneath the water's surface – ten times the length of the boat. He reached out to touch the shadowy figure before Kawelo could stop him. A monster burst from the depths of the sea. It looked almost like a shark, only bigger, with scales like a crocodile and teeth larger than anything they had ever seen. The monster dived back into the water and the boat was thrown up into the air on the churning waves. Kawelo grabbed hold of his son and pushed him to the other side of the boat to protect him from the monster. It was pointless to try and row away – Apukohai was faster.

Terrified, and quickly running out of ideas, Kawelo prayed to the gods. He asked the gods to keep him and his son safe. And at that exact moment, Apukohai opened its mouth and swallowed Kawelo whole. His son looked on in horror. But the gods heard Kawelo's prayer. The next thing Kauluiki saw was an owl flying over the horizon and swooping down close to the surface of the sea. The owl landed on the edge of the boat, and Kauluiki recognised him instantly. This was not an ordinary owl – it was the owl god, who could bring back those who had been killed before their time. More owls arrived, and more and more. Apukohai tried to leap from the water again, but each time he did, a thousand owls swooped around him and blocked out the Sun. The monster was so confused that he spat out Kawelo and fled back down to the sea's depths. Whoever heard of owls out at sea? He never returned to the surface again, preferring the predictable dark of the seafloor to the strange darkness above.

Kauluiki pulled his father from the water, relieved to find him all in one piece. With the owl god perched on the prow of their boat, they rowed all the way to Kauai. Fishermen brought the story of their adventure to shore before they had even arrived, and the tale spread around the island. Kawelo's brothers did not dare to argue with the ones who had defeated Apukohai. Kawelo, the chief, and Kauluiki danced a happy hula on the shore. And every time the little family saw an owl flying above their heads, they thanked it for protecting them from the monster of the deep.

UNDER THE SEA

What dwells beneath the ocean's waves? Ancient cultures were fascinated with beasts that lived under the sea. From enormous sea monsters to real animals like dolphins, sharks, and fish, stories about beasts showed the power of the ocean's depths and the role it played in the lives of the humans who depended on it.

Moche sea monster

The Moche people of ancient Peru made lots of vessels with fish and crabs on them, which often have legs or arms that look very human. Maybe they were impressed by the special power that crabs have to live both on the land and in the sea and craved it for themselves. This might also explain why Moche artists seem to have experimented with showing fish that had legs so that they could walk on land.

Global sea dragon

The Etruscans (who lived in ancient Italy) believed that in the seas there lived a dangerous dragon-like beast known as a 'ketos'. The ketos was usually shown with the head of a mammal and the body of a whale or dolphin. The ketos had an important role in guiding the souls of the dead across the sea and into the underworld. Objects decorated with images of this fearsome monster caught on and were traded around the world. Historians think that the ketos had an influence on dragons in places as far from the Mediterranean as ancient Afghanistan, India, and China.

Dolphins and sharks

The real-life beasts of the sea were as much of interest to ancient artists as the mythical beasts. Across the ancient world there are images of dolphins and sharks – like this shark with big teeth from ancient South America. Dolphins have always had a very close relationship with humans – the Roman author Pliny describes how he saw a dolphin on the coast of North Africa playing with humans and eating food from their hands. Another Roman author described dolphins as "the kings of the sea creatures".

Sea-goats

In Greek mythology the sea-goat was said to have been created when the gods were trying to escape an attack by the monstrous giant Typhoeus. All of the gods took the form of animals to hide from the giant – the god Aigipan took the form of a goat with the tail of a fish. The giant had almost defeated Zeus, the king of the gods, by pulling out the muscles from his legs, but Aigipan came to the rescue. To thank Aigipan, Zeus turned him into a constellation in the form of the sea-goat – it was the constellation Capricorn, which is still part of the Western zodiac today. The story was told all over the ancient world.

Seashells

One of the most ancient symbols found across the world is the coiling seashell. These objects could be used for communication, since they make a sound when air is blown in through a hole at one end. In Greek mythology, the god Triton used a magic conch shell like a trumpet to raise the sea's waves or calm them. Shells could also be made into precious objects like jewellery or carved into small containers. These shells are found across Europe and Asia but in Palestine the shells are often found with their carvings half-finished, or not yet started. This is a clue that this region is where the shell artists' workshops were – if they messed up while carving a shell, they threw it away.

KIND BEASTS

Beasts are not always fierce and cruel. They can also be kind. We know this in the modern world, of course, because we live with real life beasts in our homes and all around us in the wild. We build friendships with animals even though they are so different to us (and sometimes even because of these differences). The stories we tell about kind beasts remind us of this – they remind us that humans are not alone in the world. And they show us how much we depend on beasts who can do things that we can't. By showing us that beasts can be kind, these stories encourage us to be kinder too, and to remember that we share our planet with so many other species who have just as much right to live here as we do. These myths remind us of the role these beasts play in all of our lives.

FANGFENG'S SACRIFICE

King Yu had done something impossible. He had managed to stop the floods, which had been coming since the beginning of time. When the water flowed over the banks of the river and into the fields, the crops drowned and there was nothing left to eat. Sometimes water would continue to rise and rise until it covered the rooftops, and families had to swim from their windows to escape. People were dying – until King Yu put a stop to it.

The king lived in a palace on top of a mountain, along with the people who had fled the lands below. But not everyone could leave their lives behind. Some wanted to stay with their animals, or kept trying to farm their crops. Others were simply too old and frail to climb a mountain.

Many people had tried to turn back the water before King Yu, using barriers and walls. But he had an idea that was very different. What if, instead of working against the Earth, he worked with it? He asked the mountains for their help – and not just the mountains but the seas and the rivers and the soil and the whole of the earth. He asked the beasts of the Earth for their help too. And all of them came together to help him. The dragons dug channels so that water could flow out of the rivers to the sea, and a giant tortoise hauled all of the mud up from the bottoms of the rivers so they would hold more water. The next time the flood water came, it simply bubbled down through the channels and out into the sea. The great floods were over.

King Yu called all the beasts and people to the mountain to celebrate this victory. Eventually, all the beasts had arrived except one. Fangfeng was missing. Now that King Yu thought about it, he realised that he had not seen the beast hard at work battling the flood, like the others. Hot rage began to bubble in his belly. Fangfeng must have disobeyed him. The king called some of the dragons to him, and told them to kill Fangfeng as soon as they saw him coming up the mountain. This was the only way, King Yu thought, to punish him for his disobedience.

There was something King Yu did not know about Fangfeng. Since the flood had started, the creature had not been seen on the top of any of the four mountains. He had stayed down in the valley below, helping the people who could not leave their homes – because they were too frail or too poor to escape. When the floods came, Fangfeng used his huge body to keep the families who stayed in the valley from drowning. He helped them to rebuild their homes when the waters were lower again, and he helped them to find food when their crops had died. While King Yu was busying himself with the people on the mountaintops, Fangfeng had never forgotten those who did not have the privilege of being among them.

But although King Yu had not seen Fangfeng's kindness from his palace, other creatures had. The cranes who flew from one mountain to another had looked down and seen Fangfeng helping the people who had stayed in the valley. So when Fangfeng's ox ears appeared in the distance, the cranes flew around him in a circle, hiding him from the dragons that King Yu had sent to kill him. When Fangfeng arrived to tell the king what had happened, he was taken aback – then thanked him for his kindness. Everyone who lived at the top of the mountains climbed onto Fangfeng's back and went back down into the valley. There, safe from the flood, they rebuilt their villages. And they promised never to forget how unkind it is to leave other people behind.

FEAR OF OTHERS

When ancient people met others who lived very different lives to theirs, they sometimes responded in unkind ways. The ancient world was full of stories about people who travelled to far away lands, and found monsters and mythical beasts there. These stories, of course, were not true – the people they encountered were people, just like them. But travellers and story tellers exaggerated to find a way of understanding new people and experiences.

Meeting monsters in foreign lands

When ancient travellers went a long way from home they brought back tales of monsters. The Roman writer Pliny tells us that in ancient Africa there were beasts who had the head of a dog and the body of a human being. It wasn't easy to travel long distances or check facts back then, so writers could get away with telling tall tales! Stories like these made Romans afraid of other places rather than excited to visit.

Kamsa and Keshi

Beasts and monsters could be used as a symbol of arguments between humans, with friends or even with family members. The demon Keshi appears in this kind of story. In Hindu myth, the story goes that the God Krishna had an uncle called Kamsa. The uncle had been told that he was destined to die at the hands of his nephew, so he sent a series of demons to the house of Krishna's foster parents to try and get rid of him. Keshi was a demon in the form of an enormous horse, who could gallop at the speed of thoughts. He was no match for Krishna, though, who defeated him, as well as all the other demons that his uncle Kamsa sent.

Alexander and the dragon

Alexander the Great was a ruthless warrior who conquered ancient people from Greece to India. Like many conquering kings, Alexander was so famous that later writers came up with ever more exciting stories to tell about him. According to those who spread his legend, Alexander faced mythical beasts as well as human opponents. He arrived on an island in the Indian Ocean where a dragon was eating all of the other animals. Alexander killed the dragon, and in order to thank him, the islanders gave him an enormous rabbit, with yellow fur and a single horn in the middle of its head.

Unique bodies

It was common in the ancient world for people to call other people monsters when something about their body was different from theirs. This was the case, for example, with the Cyclops. The Cyclops was a giant with only one eye in the middle of his head. Just like in the world today, there were people in the ancient world who had one eye instead of two (or whose bodies were unique in any number of other ways). Today we are getting better at understanding that differences can be our greatest strength, rather than something to be afraid of.

This imprint was made by an ancient seal. It shows the hero Gilgamesh (centre) meeting the scorpion men at the gates of the Netherworld. They let him through because he was two-thirds a god.

Half-man, half-scorpion

The ancient Mesopotamians thought that mountains were scary places because they were so different to their own flat plains. They thought that many monstrous creatures lived there, such as human-scorpion hybrids that could kill you just by looking at you! Even though they looked scary, they had an important job to do: they guarded the gates to the Netherworld where the Sun went at night. Such an important place naturally needed powerful and terrifying guardians.

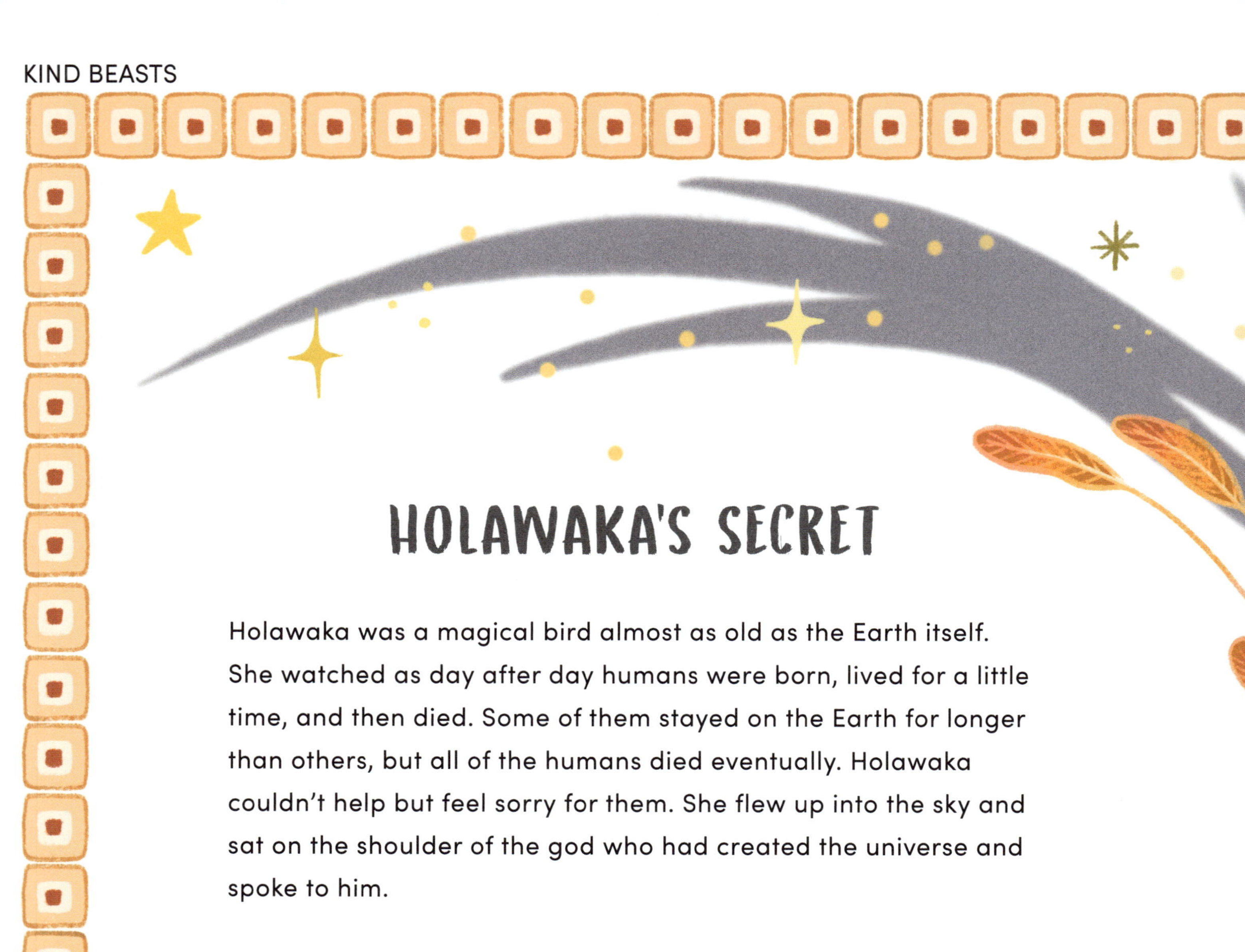

HOLAWAKA'S SECRET

Holawaka was a magical bird almost as old as the Earth itself. She watched as day after day humans were born, lived for a little time, and then died. Some of them stayed on the Earth for longer than others, but all of the humans died eventually. Holawaka couldn't help but feel sorry for them. She flew up into the sky and sat on the shoulder of the god who had created the universe and spoke to him.

"It isn't fair," Holawaka said, "that the humans are only allowed to stay on the Earth for such a short time." But the god just laughed gently, and told her that humans were not like her and the gods. Humans could not be allowed to live forever. At this, Holawaka began to cry and the god could not help feeling her sadness too. He told Holawaka to return the next night. Holawaka did as the god had asked. The next night she flew back up to the highest point of the sky, dodging through the stars as she flew. The god's voice made all the stars around them shake and tremble. "Since the fate of these tiny humans matters so much to you," the god said, "I will let you have your wish. But you must not tell any of the

other animals what I have given you." Then he told Holawaka a secret: it was possible for the humans to live forever. All they had to do was to slip off their wrinkly skins as they were approaching old age, and they would find a new young skin underneath. Holowaka could not wait to tell the humans what she had learnt.

She flew back down to the Earth where the humans lived. Several hours had now passed, and the Sun was starting to creep up from behind the horizon. The humans were still asleep, but they would soon be awake to hear what she had to tell them. She perched on one of the branches of a juniper tree and waited. But she was not alone. Next to her on the branch was a baboon, who asked, "What have you got to look so happy about, Holawaka?" Holawaka explained that the god had told her a special secret that would allow the humans to live forever. "But I can't tell you what it is," she said to the baboon, "so please don't ask me to."

The baboon, of course, did ask for Holawaka's secret. He promised that if she told him, he would teach her how to climb to the top of any of the trees in Ethiopia. But Holawaka had wings and could fly to the highest point in the sky. She did not need to trade the secret that the god had given her for climbing lessons from the baboon. He gave up asking and swung away.

Down below, in the shade of the juniper tree, a lion was waking up. He shook his head and enormous black mane. "Did I hear that right, Holawaka, that the god told you a special secret that will allow the humans to live forever?" Holawaka was an honest kind of a bird, so she told the lion that this was true. "Will you tell it to me," the lion asked, "if I promise to teach you how to be the king of the animals?" Holawaka thought about this for a moment. The idea of being the king of all the animals was tempting… but she could not agree. And besides, she knew that she was already the god's favourite animal, so she did not need the animals to call her 'king'.

By now the sun had almost risen. The other animals were making their way into their burrows to hide away from the warmth of the day. But Holawaka was still sitting on the branch of the juniper tree. She felt her tummy start to rumble – she had not eaten anything since night had fallen. Suddenly the fact that she was hungry was all that she could think about.

At that moment, a snake slithered its way up the tree. In its fangs, the snake held the remains of its last meal. Holawaka's eyes lit up. "Snake!" she called out, forgetting what the god had asked of her, "will you share your food with me if I tell you a secret?" The snake hissed and brought the food close enough to Holawaka that she could almost taste it. "The secret is from the god who created the universe," Holawaka added.

The snake gave Holawaka a bite of food, and without stopping to think, she gobbled it up. Then she told him the god's secret. The snake did something Holawaka could not have imagined. He decided to test out the god's secret. He slipped out of his old skin and found that just underneath it, a new one had been growing. The humans never did learn the god's secret. But to this day snakes slip out of their skins when they grow old and wrinkled, as Holawaka taught them to do.

BEASTS WE LOVE

Not all beasts in the ancient world were scary monsters. Many ancient people kept pets in their homes, just like we do today. Some of these animals had jobs to do. They herded sheep and cows, helped ancient people to hunt other animals, and guarded their homes. Others were kept as friends, like our pets today. There were many different opinions on how animals should be treated in the ancient world. Some ancient people loved animals so much that they were vegetarians, and refused to eat them. Others worshipped them as gods and goddesses. Some thought that they were less important than humans, and could be cruel to them.

Dogs

Today the most common type of pet in the world is a dog – and that was true in the ancient world as well. Dogs helped ancient people with farming and hunting, but they also had very close friendships with them. In the ancient Greek poem the *Odyssey*, the hero Odysseus travels for ten long years to get back to his home. When he arrives back at his palace, he arrives in disguise so that he can see what has happened in his absence. Although his wife, his son, and most of his friends do not recognise him, his faithful dog Argos does.

This carved bear has a secret. The rope around its neck is not only a sign of its captivity, it hides a hinge. Ancient Romans used vessels like this to keep their bath oils in.

Unusual pets

Dogs were not the only animals kept as pets in the ancient world – some ancient people's choices were a little more unusual. The Romans kept pets like birds and rabbits in their homes – but also bears and monkeys. The Roman Emperor Valentinian owned two pet bears named Goldflake and Innocence. Sadly, bears were also used in circus acts where they were not treated well. The ancient Egyptians are famous for their love of cats, but they also kept baboons as pets and cheetahs that they walked on a lead with a collar like dogs!

Love/hate relationship

Even people who did not keep animals as pets in their homes were intrigued by images of animals, including ones that could cause as much harm as good. Many ancient objects were made in the shapes of animals, especially ones that were considered brave. This container from Iran is made in the shape of a wild boar, a fierce animal that destroyed crops and could attack humans if threatened. The stripes show its thick, bristly fur.

Baku

In ancient Japanese legend, there is a much-loved creature that looks a little bit like a tapir but with an elephant's trunk, called Baku. This beast has a very special job. Anyone who has a nightmare simply has to call out to the Baku, "Come and eat my dream, Baku!" and the creature will come to their bedroom and devour the nightmare. This made Baku popular! But the creature could also be dangerous. Some say that if the Baku was still hungry after it had eaten up the person's nightmares, it could gobble up their good dreams too.

A monster's pet monster

Mythical beasts themselves sometimes kept mythical beasts of their own as pets. Greek myth tells the story of Geryon, a giant with three bodies, who was killed by Hercules. Hercules had been tasked with stealing Geryon's herd of magical cows. Geryon had a pet called Orthrus, a dog with two heads. Orthrus was the brother of a three-headed dog called Cerebus, who had the special task of guarding the gates of the Underworld. When Hercules came to steal Geryon's cattle, Orthrus bravely tried to protect them and his owner, but was killed while defending them.

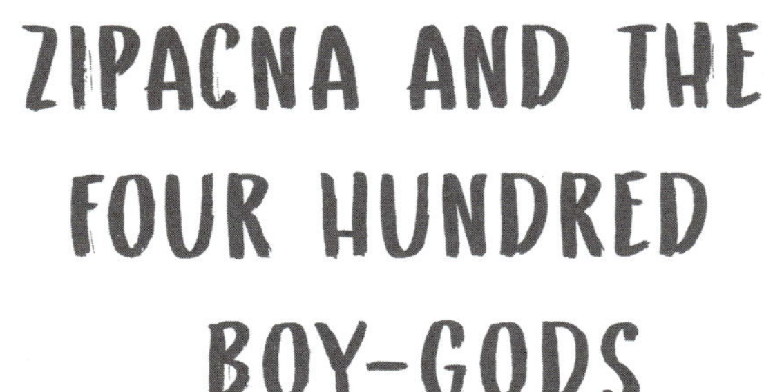

ZIPACNA AND THE FOUR HUNDRED BOY-GODS

It never seemed fair to Zipacna that everyone thought he was evil. It was his brother, Cabrakan, who made earthquakes happen when he got angry. But Zipacna had never caused any earthquakes. He had raised the mountains from the earth back when the world was new, though. And he never got tired of talking about it. In the middle of any conversation, Zipacna would stop and say, "Did you know that I created the mountains?" The other gods and goddesses found it boring. So Zipacna spent most of his time alone, basking in the sunshine on the sandy beach.

One day Zipacna heard the sound of boys muttering amongst themselves. It sounded like they were upset about something. Zipacna turned around and saw the Four Hundred Boys on the beach behind him. What was this group of gods doing down here? The trunk of a large tree lay on the floor in the middle of them. "What are you doing here?" Zipacna asked.

 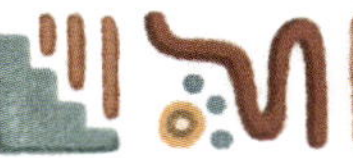  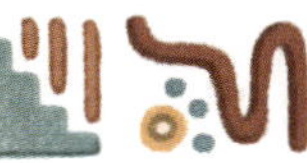 

But the Four Hundred Boys did not listen. "We already know that you raised the mountains from the Earth, Zipacna – you don't need to tell us again!" one of them shouted. But Zipacna could tell from the tone of his voice that the boy did not really believe that he had raised the mountains.

Ceramic crocodile
c. 4th century

The Mayans both worshipped and feared the crocodile. It symbolised new beginnings and even life itself, but as American crocodiles can grow up to 4.5m (15 ft) long, encounters with this reptile could be dangerous.

Another boy spoke: "We are building a hut down here on the beach. This tree will stand in the middle of the hut to keep it stable." But the Four Hundred Boys – even though there were four hundred of them – were not able to lift up the tree trunk that they had cut down. Zipacna slithered his way up the beach towards them. "Let me assist you," he said. "It will be no trouble for me, after all it was me who rais–" He stopped himself from speaking just before he finished saying that it was he who had raised the mountains from the Earth.

Before long, the tree trunk was exactly where they needed it. Zipacna really was as strong as he had always said he was. The Four Hundred Boys set to work chopping smaller pieces of wood and collecting together leaves to build their hut. But something started to worry them. Perhaps it was not right, they thought, for a creature to have so much strength? There was no telling what else Zipacna might be able to do. A whisper went around the Four Hundred Boys. Perhaps it would be better to kill Zipacna, now that they knew how powerful he was? One by one, the boys agreed with each other that this had to be done. Some of them felt a little sorry, since Zipacna had been so helpful to them. But their fear got the better of them.

The Four Hundred Boys told Zipacna that they needed another favour. "We need to dig a huge hole in the sand, so that this tree trunk can stand upright and support the hut," they told him. They did not tell him their plan to push the tree trunk over, so that it would fall across the hole and kill Zipacna once he had started digging. But the crocodile was not so easily fooled. For years the gods and goddesses had been trying to avoid hearing the story of how he raised the mountains. He knew a lie when he heard one.

Without the Four Hundred Boys noticing, Zipacna dug an extra tunnel that led away from the one they had asked him to dig. He hid inside the extra tunnel, then as the boys let the tree trunk fall sideways over the hole (working together for once), Zipacna

cried out as if he had been hit. To make sure that they believed that they had killed him, Zipacna gave three of his scales and one of his claws to some ants who were passing through in the sand. The ants took the scales and claw to the Four Hundred Boys, who were convinced that their plan had worked.

Then, as the Four Hundred Boys were celebrating their success, Zipacna lifted his body out from under the sand. He used all of his enormous strength – and he was so big that it looked like mountains were rising up from the beach. He swished his tail, and the rest of the hut that the Four Hundred Boys had built collapsed onto the sand. No one would dare tell Zipacna not to boast about raising the mountains from the Earth ever again.

CATCHING A UNICORN

For years the mother goddess had refused to send any rain to the old king's land. The king's people were hungry and thirsty, because they could not grow any food to eat. Every morning, they gathered in front of his palace. Their mouths were dry, and they could barely speak. But their thirst made them brave. "You must do something, king," they shouted, "anything to make the rain come again!" But he did not know what to do.

The king gathered together the wisest people in the land and asked for their advice. One woman had an idea. "In the forest at the edge of our land," she explained, "lives a kind and gentle creature that the mother goddess loves most of all." Someone else tried to interrupt, to tell the wise woman that the creature would never leave the forest, but she continued. "It will not be easy, but if you can bring the creature here, then the mother goddess will send us rain again." The king was not sure that he understood the wise woman's suggestion. But the ways of the gods were mysterious, and he had no choice but to trust her.

When he asked what the creature looked like, she told him that it looked like a horse, except that its fur was red and it had a single horn in the middle of its head. It was called a unicorn. Even though the king had never seen a creature like this, he set off to try and catch it. He went as far as he dared to go into the forest's dark depths. Here the trees were so close together that he had to squeeze through the gaps, and it was so dark he could hardly see his own feet. Suddenly he saw a glint of light – it was the unicorn's horn. He pulled out his net and started to run towards the light. But before he had moved three steps the creature had gone.

The king went to the forest day after day. Day after day he returned without the unicorn. His people were still hungry. When he lay in his bed at night, he could hear thousands of tummies rumbling. He had to do something. The next morning, when he went into the forest, he took his bow and arrow with him. The wise woman had not told him that he needed to bring the unicorn back to the palace alive. If the unicorn could not be caught, then he would kill it, and bring it back as an offering to the mother goddess.

Today, something was different in the forest. In the middle of the narrow track that he usually followed as far as he dared, was a little girl. She was standing with her hands on her hips and a determined look on her face. The king did not need to speak to her to know that she did not intend to let him pass. Instead, he asked the girl her name, and demanded that she explain what she was doing in the dark forest at the very edge of the land. "My name," the girl replied, "is Aadhya. I've heard all about you, king, and I am here to stop you from doing a terrible thing." She gestured towards the bow and arrow that the king was carrying. "It is wrong to kill a kind creature who has done nothing to harm you," she said, looking fierce.

Suddenly the king felt a sense of shame. Aadhya was right. It wasn't the unicorn's fault that his people were hungry and thirsty. His cheeks burned hot and tears fell from his eyes. "I don't want to hurt the unicorn," the king said to Aadhya, "I just don't know what else to do." The little girl gestured for the king to follow her down the narrow track, and he did. "Have you tried," she suggested, "simply asking the unicorn to help?" The king shook his head. Asking the creature for help? It seemed so simple, too simple to work. But Aadhya did not wait for him to agree to her plan. "It is better to ask the unicorn for help than to try to force it to come against its will," she said. She clicked her tongue against her teeth three times. And to the king's surprise the unicorn appeared.

The unicorn approached the girl and lowered its head into her hands. Aadhya spoke quietly. She explained how the mother goddess had refused to send any rain to the king's land, and the unicorn was their only hope. The unicorn paused, then nodded. The girl patted the unicorn's nose, then led the way out of the forest. The king walked behind the girl and the unicorn, his mouth wide open in amazement. By the time they arrived back at the king's palace, every cloud in the sky had burst open with rain. Rivers ran through the streets, and the king's people had brought out cups to fill with water so they could drink. Flowers and crops burst out in the fields, and everyone knew that the mother goddess was pleased. The king thanked Aadhya for her help, and promised he would never forget to ask for help instead of trying to solve a problem by force. The king had learnt that sometimes even the biggest problems have simple solutions.

THE INDUS VALLEY

The Indus river flows from the Himalayan mountains for hundreds of miles until it reaches the Arabian Sea. On the banks of this river, in what is now Tibet, India, Pakistan, and Kashmir, lived the ancient people of the Indus Valley. Their towns and cities were built from mud bricks and expertly planned out, with wide streets so that elephants and chariots pulled by bulls could pass each other by. High walls meant that the Indus people were well protected from attack. Hardly any weapons have been found by archaeologists in this area, so we can assume that they lived very peaceful lives.

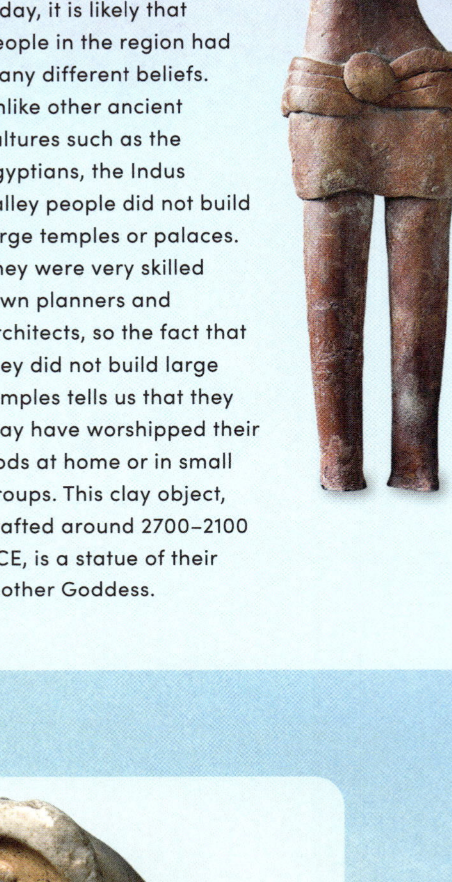

Ideas and beliefs

Not much is known about the religion of the people who lived in the Indus Valley. Like today, it is likely that people in the region had many different beliefs. Unlike other ancient cultures such as the Egyptians, the Indus Valley people did not build large temples or palaces. They were very skilled town planners and architects, so the fact that they did not build large temples tells us that they may have worshipped their gods at home or in small groups. This clay object, crafted around 2700–2100 BCE, is a statue of their Mother Goddess.

Goods for sale

As well as eating the food they produced, Indus Valley people sold extra food and other goods at markets in major cities. They didn't have tame horses, so people rode on bulls – like this woman is doing in the statue (left). Harappa was the first of these ancient cities to be excavated by archaeologists. They found a marketplace and evidence that people from other regions came from far away to buy Indus Valley goods. Indus Valley people don't seem to have used money, so they probably traded directly using objects they made, like this carved sheep (right).

Mystery writing

One of the reasons we know little about the religious views and other important parts of the lives of Indus Valley people, is that we cannot read their writing. We have lots of examples of their writing and the letters they used, but we have not been able to decipher it. Thousands of seals have been found in the Indus Valley region, most of them showing animals like buffalos (and sometimes mythical beasts) with a line of letters or text. We think that these would have been attached to goods in the marketplace – perhaps so buyers could tell who had made the products. If we could decipher this language, we would know a lot more about this fascinating ancient culture!

Animal toys

The Indus Valley was a fun place to live if you were a kid – archaeologists have found lots of children's toys, mostly in the form of animals. These included miniature models of oxen made in terracotta, which could be attached to a toy plough. Objects with a serious purpose were often decorated with animals too, like the urns that were used in burials.

Separated statues

The artists of the Indus Valley were some of the first portrait makers in the world. This bronze sculpture of a girl (below left) was made around 2300–1750 BCE, in a city called Mohenjo Daro (in what is now Pakistan). A difficult choice had to be made between the bronze girl and this stone sculpture of a priest (below right). When the British colonised India, they moved these two statues away from where they belonged to New Delhi, the capital of British-occupied India. The government of Pakistan later asked for the statues to be returned to where they were found – but were told they could only choose one. The stone priest was returned to Pakistan while the girl remained in India.

Sharing myths

The Indus Valley people traded with other ancient cultures including the Parthians (from what is now Iran) and the ancient Greeks. The Greeks said that one of their gods, Dionysus the god of theatre and wine, had come from India. These cultures left their mark on Indus Valley art too. This seal, called the Pashupati seal, shows a half-human, half-buffalo monster. Some people think it shows an early version of the Hindu god Shiva, who is also known as Pashupati. Others think it is a horned monster who fought the famous Mesopotamian hero Gilgamesh. This character crossover shows us how ancient people shared stories and ideas.

THE MOON WOMAN AND THE MOON RABBIT

High up in the sky, nestled between the stars and enclosed safely inside the Moon, there lived the Moon Woman. The Moon Woman was very kind. Every night she looked down to the Earth and saw something that broke her heart. A drought had come, and the humans could not grow rice to eat. They didn't know of other ways to get food. They were getting so thin she could see their bones from up in the sky. Even worse was the way they were treating each other. They began to steal what little food their neighbours had, and cheated each other at the marketplace.

The Moon Woman decided something had to be done. She leapt out of the Moon, diving into the night sky. She swam through the stars and clouds. As she swam she transformed herself. Everyone on Earth looked at the Moon and saw the Moon Woman every night. She did not want them to recognise her. She disguised herself as one of the hungry old men from the village, and asked the animals for help.

The first animal she saw was a red fox, sleeping under a fig tree. He opened one eye grumpily. "Please, red fox," the Moon Woman said in the voice of the old man, "could you help me? I am very hungry." The red fox was getting ready to turn around and go

back to sleep, when the Moon Woman said, "I have heard that only the most clever creatures know how to find something to eat around here." The fox could not resist a chance to show off. He led the Moon Woman high up into the mountains, where it was far too cold for humans to go safely. Near the top, he crouched down on the banks of a narrow stream and caught three large fish in his paws. No humans had been here, so there were plenty of fish. He gave the fish to the Moon Woman – and tried not to act too pleased when she said he was as clever as she had heard.

On her way back down the mountain, the Moon Woman spotted a monkey. "I'm very hungry," she said. "Could you help me find some food?" The monkey was about to tell her to go away and find her own food, when she added: "They tell me that you are strong enough to climb the tallest trees," she said, "but I'm not sure I believe it." The monkey wanted to prove this was true, so he set off swinging from branch to branch. It was far too high for humans to climb, so there was plenty of fruit at the top. When the monkey came back down, he was carrying three starfruits. He gave them to the Moon Woman. Before she could thank him, he said, "You see, I really am as strong as people say!"

Jade rabbit

c. 1300 BCE

Stories about a rabbit are told in Vietnam, China, Korea, and Japan. Pendants made from pale, luminous jade have been made in these countries since ancient times, to remind people of the rabbit's incredible selflessness.

The Moon Woman accepted the monkey's fruit and started walking towards the nearest human village. But then she stumbled upon another animal.

A rabbit was blocking her path. "I am very hungry," she said, "please can you help me find some food?" Unlike the other animals, the rabbit agreed immediately. There was just one problem: she did not have any food to give. She could not fish from a stream, or climb a tree. There was only one thing she could think of that would feed the hungry old man. The rabbit spoke quietly and nervously. "M-m-make a fire," she said, "and I will prepare you a meal." The Moon Woman did as she had asked. The rabbit stepped back and took a run up. She was leaping into the flames to roast herself, when the Moon Woman cried "STOP!" The Moon Woman transformed out of her disguise and caught the rabbit in the middle of her big leap. They stared at each other. "Were you really willing to give up your life for me?" the Moon Woman asked. But the rabbit was so shocked that she could not respond.

Together the rabbit and the Moon Woman walked, and hopped, into the village. They gave the fish and the starfruit to the people, and told them how to find more. From that day onwards the humans worked together with the animals so that there was always enough food to go around. They never stole from each other again.

But the Moon Woman wanted to give a bigger reward to the rabbit. She wanted to make sure that she could never do anything to harm herself again. "Since you were so kind, I will take you with me to the Moon," she said. And she took the rabbit in her arms and set off back towards the Moon, where they have lived together ever since. Even now, when people look at the Moon late at night, they can still see the woman and the rabbit looking back at them.

HARNESSING THE POWER OF BEASTS

Some beasts have extra-special relationships with humans. They work together with humans, helping them to achieve their goals. Sometimes they do this by choice, because they know it is easier to work together than it is to work alone. When those beasts could not be convinced to help out of friendship, they were compelled by force. There is a secret to these stories, though. And it is a secret that humans do not often want to admit: no one is all-powerful. We can't do everything on our own. On top of that, there is something much more powerful than humans, which is nature itself. These stories remind us that the position that humans have in the universe comes about by working together with others. What's more, our position in the universe can change at any moment.

PAZUZU AND LAMASHTU

To his great surprise, Hanpu, who was the god of evil, had one very kind son. Pazuzu was a demon like the rest of Hanpu's children, but unlike the others he thought it was wrong to harm the humans. Whenever one of his brothers and sisters would decide to meddle in the lives of the humans, he would plead with his fellow demons to stop and to leave them alone. He also controlled one of the winds, the one that blew from the south-west. And he used this to his advantage.

The humans rarely caught sight of Pazuzu. He had wings that flew so fast on the winds that he became invisible. If they had seen him, they might not have recognised him as a god. He had the body of a dog – though he had

scales where most dogs have fur – the talons of an eagle, and the tail of a scorpion. And his face was somewhere between that of a dog and a human, though he had pointy horns that stuck out from the centre of his forehead. But even though the humans did not see Pazuzu, they knew what he did to protect them.

Meanwhile, something terrible was happening to human mothers. On the first night after they had given birth to their babies, they had terrible nightmares. They would dream that a vicious demon came into the room where they were sleeping. All of the mothers agreed on what the demon looked like. She had hair all over her body, the head of a lioness with the ears of a donkey, and long bird-like talons instead of feet. Some of the mothers knew her name: Lamashtu. She appeared exactly the same way in each of their dreams. And when each of the mothers woke the next morning, they would find their babies gone.

This was all the humans knew about Lamashtu. But Pazuzu knew her well. And Pazuzu knew exactly how to stop her. Lamashtu was not afraid of humans, but she was afraid of demons. And even though Pazuzu was much kinder than his demon brothers and sisters were, he could look every bit as scary as they did. That night he crept into the house of one of the women who had just had a baby in a nearby village. He hid himself under the bed where the mother and her baby were sleeping. And he waited for Lamashtu to come.

As soon as the sun had vanished from the sky, Lamashtu came, exactly as Pazuzu had guessed. The human mother tossed and turned in her sleep, as the monster appeared to her in a nightmare. Lamashtu reached out her long fingers to grab the tiny baby and right at that moment, Pazuzu leapt out from under the bed. He contorted his face into the fierce expression that he had seen his brothers and sisters make – even though it did not suit him at all. He roared with a terrifying growl that even his father, the god of evil, would have been proud of. Lamashtu turned and fled out of the house into the dark night.

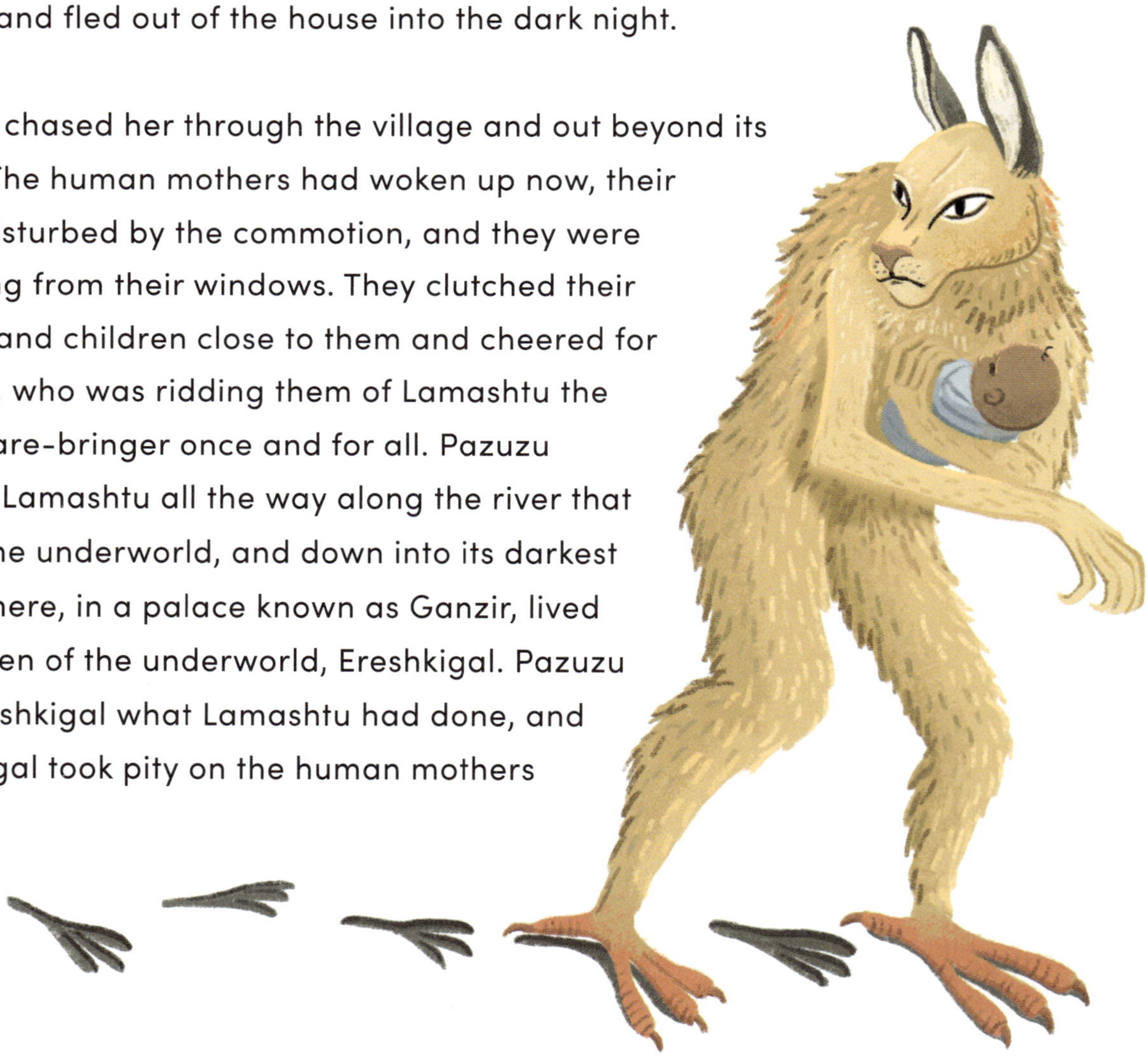

Pazuzu chased her through the village and out beyond its gates. The human mothers had woken up now, their sleep disturbed by the commotion, and they were watching from their windows. They clutched their babies and children close to them and cheered for Pazuzu, who was ridding them of Lamashtu the nightmare-bringer once and for all. Pazuzu chased Lamashtu all the way along the river that led to the underworld, and down into its darkest cave. There, in a palace known as Ganzir, lived the queen of the underworld, Ereshkigal. Pazuzu told Ereshkigal what Lamashtu had done, and Ereshkigal took pity on the human mothers

who had lost so many of their children. She called to her gate-keeper Bitu, and told him to lock each of the seven bolts on the gates to the underworld to keep Lamashtu inside. The humans might have nightmares about Lamashtu for the rest of time, but she would never leave the underworld to harm them again.

Pazuzu carving

8th century BC

Mesopotamian people wore amulets to ward off the demons they were afraid of. This stone amulet of Pazuzu reminded them that some demons were on the side of humans and could protect them from the vengeful ones.

The human mothers never forgot what Pazuzu did for them. And now that they had seen him running through their village, they knew what the creature looked like. They took pieces of stone and carved images of Pazuzu into them, and hung them from the rooftops of their homes. That way, they thought, if Lamashtu ever did return, she would see the face of Pazuzu and be frightened, just as she had been that night when she was chased away. The human mothers would never know that it was not their stone images of Pazuzu that kept her away but the queen of the underworld – but either way, Lamashtu never returned to their village again.

GREAT GUARDIANS

One of the most important jobs that beasts – both real and mythical – could do for ancient humans was to guard them. Beasts could guard families, homes, gates, and even the afterlife in order to keep humans safe. Sometimes mythical beasts even guarded certain places from humans, stopping them from going into dark forests, for example, or from disrupting the homes of other creatures.

The dragons of Babylon

In ancient Mesopotamia (modern Iraq) there stood a city called Babylon. The city was surrounded by high walls, to keep the people there safe. The walls were decorated with images of beasts, both mythical and real. These animals included lions, dragons, and other creatures that were sacred to the god Marduk, who was the protector of the city. One of the dragons, called Mushkushshu (above), was part-lion, part-viper, with talons like a bird of prey. According to legend, the dragon had been defeated by Marduk and became his servant, helping to protect Babylon.

The kings of Assyria loved Lamassu so much they carved it all over their palaces and temples from the 9th to the 7th centuries BCE. Each scuplture could weigh up to 40 tonnes (45 tons).

Lamassu

Ancient Mesopotamian people received protection from another mythical beast, Lamassu. This creature had a human head, the body of a bull, and wings. Statues of them were placed at the entrance to homes and cities, to protect the people who lived there. They were also engraved into clay tablets which were buried in the ground doorways. In earlier history humans asked for protection from a creature called Lamma, who had the body of a human (often a woman), and the wings of a bird and was sometimes also part-lion. Later Lamassu took over this role, but you can tell from the sounds in their names that the two creatures were related.

Guardians of tombs

In ancient China many people thought that humans had two parts of their souls – the hun and the po. When the person had died, the hun was said to leave their body, but the po stayed behind with the body of the person inside the tomb. When someone was buried, their friends and family would leave gifts behind of all the things that the po might need. This would include cutlery to eat with, musical instruments to keep themselves entertained and sometimes weapons. Many families also left a guardian beast, to protect the po in the tomb. These were made to look fierce and scary and usually had fangs and horns.

Guarding gone wrong

In ancient West Africa, the Krachi people asked for the protection of their creator god Wulbari. In one story, a flesh-eating bird called Animabri was killing humans. Wulbari called all the beasts together and told them that no one was to harm the humans, including Animabri. The bird scoffed, but obeyed. Then he gave his dog a special task: to take a potion to the humans so they could bring back to life the people Animabri had killed. On the way, the dog was distracted by an enormous bone lying on the side of the road. While she ate, a goat took the potion and sprinkled it all over the grass. And that was the reason humans do not come back to life after they have died, but grass returns every year when the rains come.

Protectors of children

For the ancient Egyptians, childbirth and childhood were the most dangerous time in a person's life. A god called Bes was responsible for protecting people during this time – but he did not do this task alone. He did it with the help of lots of different beasts, including lions and crocodiles. In this statue, Bes is wearing a lion head on his chest and he even has round, upright ears like a lion.

River guardian

In Hindu mythology, the guardian of gateways, doorways, and thresholds is a water creature called Makara. These beasts are often found at the entrance to temples. At first Makara was usually shown as part-elephant and part-fish, seal, or snake. In later art the creature was also shown looking more like a river crocodile, a dangerous animal that people travelling along rivers were afraid of. In myths, Makara is often ridden by goddesses of the rivers, like Ganga (the goddess of the Ganges river), or Varuna, the god of the ocean.

THE RIDDLE OF THE SPHINX

The Sphinx was the guardian of the gates in the city of Thebes. She came from a long line of guardians. Her father Orthrus was a two-headed dog who guarded the cattle of Geryon – a three-bodied giant who lived in the land where the sun sets. But the Sphinx looked nothing like her father. She had the head of a woman, with dark brown curly hair, the body of a lion, and the wings of an enormous bird.

It had been the Sphinx's job to guard the gates of Thebes for longer than anyone could remember. Even the oldest people in the city struggled to say when she had arrived. Occasionally an old woman would say that her grandmother had told her that it was the goddess Hera, queen of the gods, who had brought the Sphinx from Ethiopia, where she was born, to Thebes. But then an old man would disagree, and say that it was the god Ares – the god of strength and war – who had brought the Sphinx to the city. The one thing everyone agreed on, though, was that the Sphinx was excellent at her job.

Super sphinx

The Great Sphinx of Giza is a huge statue in Egypt. Carved in around 2500 BCE, it is still one of the world's largest statues. Like the sphinx in the myth, it has a lion's body and a human face, which may have been based on the face of the pharoah Khafre.

In fact, the Sphinx was such a good guardian of the gate that it had been years and years since anyone had entered Thebes at all. You see, before she would allow anyone to enter the city, the Sphinx would ask them to answer a riddle. And no one could enter the gates to the city of Thebes unless they could answer it. For as long as anyone could remember, the Sphinx had been asking the same riddle. "What walks on four legs in the morning, two legs in the afternoon, and three legs at night?" No one had ever found the answer.

Each time someone answered the riddle incorrectly, the Sphinx would tear them into little pieces. And soon, anyone who wanted to approach the gates of Thebes had to wade through piles of bones to reach them. No one could ever have guessed that one day the riddle would be answered – but one day it was.

There had been a plague in Thebes that year. All of the Thebans who lived in the city longed for someone to come through the gates bringing a cure. But no one ever came – the riddle remained unanswered. The Thebans were so desperate for someone to come and help them that they promised that whoever could answer the riddle correctly would become the king of Thebes. But still no one entered the city.

No one, that is, until a man named Oedipus arrived. Oedipus had been born in Thebes a long time ago, but his father had sent him away from the city. When he was just a baby, his father had taken him up into the mountains, tied his feet together so that he could not crawl away, and left him there. He had heard an oracle say that Oedipus would force his father off the throne and replace him as king. But Oedipus had not died as his father had imagined a baby would, out on the mountain tops all alone. He had been picked up by a shepherd, who had raised him as if he were his own son. And except for the fact that his feet were still swollen from when his father had tied them together all those years ago, it was almost impossible to tell that any of this had ever happened to Oedipus at all.

Oedipus waded through the bones and looked up at the Sphinx perched on top of the gate. He gulped, loudly, realising that he would only have one chance to answer the riddle correctly. "What walks on four legs in the morning, two legs in the afternoon, and three legs at night?" she asked (the Sphinx got straight to the point, she did

not like to make friendly conversation with the humans who approached the gate, in case they got the riddle wrong and she had to kill them). But Oedipus did not even pause to think about it. "Humans," he said – "a human being crawls on four legs as a baby, then walks on two legs as an adult, and uses a walking stick as their third leg when they reach old age."

The Sphinx was so shocked and surprised to hear the correct answer to her riddle that she dropped from her perch and died instantly. Oedipus walked through the gate and into the city of Thebes, where he became king just as the oracle had said that he would. But nothing in his life would ever again be as easy as giving the answer to the Sphinx's riddle.

DIVINE FELINES

Cats have been living alongside humans for 12,000 years. Because of their ability to hunt mice that would eat our grain, they became useful to humans. Cats used this (and their cuteness) to their advantage, convincing humans to feed them and look after them. The ancient world is full of stories that show us that ancient people loved their pet cats as much as – or maybe even more than – we do today. Some ancient people even worshipped cats as if they were gods.

Egypt's love of cats

Cats were worshipped as god-like in ancient Egypt. Gods and goddesses like Bastet, Mafdet, and Mut were often depicted with cats, or even as half-human and half-cat themselves. And it was not just mythical or divine cats but ordinary cats that were praised. The ancient Egyptians thanked cats for hunting snakes and for protecting the pharaoh. One ancient Egyptian text even says that cats are as important to humans as the Sun. After they had died, cats were often mummified and buried like humans and some of these cat mummies have survived to the present day. Other ancient people knew that cats were the Egyptians' weakness. The Persians once lined up a row of cats in front of their army. The Egyptians refused to fight out of fear of hurting the cats.

Two tails

In early Japan, there was a group of supernatural beings called nekomata cats. People believed that when pet cats grew old they could transform into these supernatural creatures. Mysterious stories were told about them. Some said that they could go up into the mountains and change into human form. Others said that these creatures could grow as large as a wild boar and could even eat humans. There was only one way that ancient people could tell a friendly house cat apart from a scary nekomata. Cats who were not dangerous only had one tail, but nekomata had two. Cats had to be treated well. If a cat had been abused or neglected by a human but lived to old age, it would become an even more fierce nekomata.

Muezza

It is said that Muhammad, the Prophet of Islam, loved his pet cat Muezza very much. One story tells us that the Prophet awoke one morning to the sound of the call to prayer, letting him know that it was time to offer the first of his five daily prayers. As he got dressed and prepared himself to pray, he noticed that his cat Muezza was fast asleep on the sleeve of the robe he was about to put on. Instead of waking up the cat, the Prophet cut off the sleeve, leaving the cat undisturbed. Then he put on the rest of his robe and prayed.

Snow leopard

Aq Bars was a giant snow leopard with wings who appears in the myths of the Barsils. These ancient people were warriors who lived between the Black Sea and the Caspian Sea. They were nomadic, so they moved around a lot, taking their stories with them. Aq Bars is still talked about today in different places where the ancient Barsils used to live. It even appears on the flag of the Republic of Tatarstan, part of Russia.

Underwater panther

Indigenous people in North America and Canada tell stories about a creature known as the underwater panther called Mishipeshu. It has the head and front paws of a large cat, but is covered in scales like a fish. It also has huge spikes running along its tail, which looks like the tail of a dragon. Some say that this ancient creature still lives in the deepest part of Lake Superior, and that it is the leader of all of the other creatures that live in the water. Others tell the story differently, and say that the underwater panther is in charge of the underworld and the leader of the snakes. It is the equal and opposite force to the Thunderbirds, who are the leaders of all of the creatures of the air.

Jaguar goddesses

Wild cats and especially spotted jaguars were very important to the people of ancient central America. The first people to live in Mexico, the Olmec, may have carved this stone statue of a jaguar god as far back at the 9th century BCE. The Maya also worshipped many jaguar gods. These included the gods of war, trade, riches, and dark magic, and the goddess of midwifery (helping women give birth). Jaguar gods and goddesses had special responsibility over the underworld and the night-time, as jaguars like to come out at night.

ARALEZ AND THE POWER OF LIFE AND DEATH

Ara was the king of Armenia as well as a very handsome man. He was so handsome that people stopped and stared at him in the street. People regularly felt like they were in love with him based on his looks alone. In fact, he was so handsome that Semiramis, the queen of Assyria, had started a war.

Semiramis had asked Ara to marry her more times than she could remember and each time he had refused. The queen did not like feeling rejected. She wanted to hurt Ara, so that he would feel how much she was hurt. She gathered together the fiercest soldiers in all of Assyria and went to war. She gave her army only one command before she led them to the battlefield: "Do not kill King Ara, bring him to me alive."

The Assyrian and Armenian armies met with a great crash of spears and chariot wheels. Lives were lost, and many of the soldiers were badly hurt. But the queen was so consumed with her own hurt that she did not think about the soldiers or their families.

The war had been going on for what felt like an eternity, when the queen suddenly stopped fighting. Something had caught her eye: a body, lying in the middle of the battlefield. She recognised him immediately. It was King Ara. The queen started to cry, and her sobs were so loud that they shook the battlefield and – just for a moment – stopped the fighting. The Assyrian soldiers surrounded her first, wondering why their queen was sobbing. Then the Armenian soldiers gathered around the body of their king. They all stared at the lifeless body.

"The one thing I asked of you," Semiramis sobbed, "was not to kill King Ara." She demanded to know who had killed him, but no one stepped forward. The soldiers began to turn on each other to take revenge.

Semiramis realised in that moment what she had done wrong. She called to her soldiers to stop. There was just one hope left. The queen knew of a creature who might be able to help her and she sent up a prayer. In the sky, a magical being appeared. It looked like a wolf, its fur white like snow, but it had golden wings on its back. The Armenian soldiers recognised the creature immediately. Some of them knelt on the floor and laid down their weapons as a sign of respect. It was Aralez.

One of the Armenian soldiers shouted, "Aralez comes when a soldier has been wrongly killed!" An Assyrian soldier said, "Aralez can undo injustices." Semiramis spoke: "I'm sorry," she said, to the gods but also to the Armenian soldiers. "I should never have started this war." Then she called all of the Assyrian and Armenian soldiers together. She asked them to raise King Ara up to the sky, where Aralez could reach him. They worked together, not stopping until they had built a tall tower. By the time they had finished building, making jokes and swapping stories as they went along, the soldiers from the two sides had become friends.

Four soldiers carried the body of King Ara to the top of the tower. At the bottom of the tower each Assyrian and Armenian prayed to their own gods, asking for Aralez's help. But the soldiers need not have worried. Aralez had already set to work. Gently, he nuzzled up to King Ara's body, and licked each of his wounds until they were healed. The battlefield fell silent, and all of the soldiers watched as Aralez worked.

Eventually, after what seemed like hours the king started to move. At first it was only his fingers and toes that came back to life, but slowly the rest of his body did too. All of a sudden, King Ara stood up at the top of the tower and waved – and the battlefield below erupted with a huge cheer. Aralez flew off, asking for nothing in return. But Semiramis had learned her lesson. It was not possible, she now knew, to inspire love through war – and it was foolish ever to try and force another person to love you. She promised Ara that she would never go to war with his kingdom ever again. And she wished him good luck – in war and in love.

SLEIPNIR AND HERMOD IN THE AFTERLIFE

Something terrible had happened to Hermod: his brother Baldr had died. Hermod and Baldr were sons of the god Odin, and gods were not yet used to the idea that dying was part of life. In their golden fortress in the sky, Asgard, all the gods and goddesses wept for Baldr. The goddess Frigg, the mother of Baldr and Hermod, promised all the love her heart could give to anyone who could bring Baldr back from the dead. Hermod volunteered.

Niflheim was created back when the world was new. It was a place of mist and ice, where everything bad had come from. It was ruled by the goddess Hel. Hermod only knew two things about this distant realm of the dead: it had walls so high that not even a god could climb them, and a cockerel lived there that would only crow at the end of the world. It did not seem like a welcoming place.

Hermod's father Odin brought out his steed Sleipnir, an enormous grey horse with eight legs. Hermod would have preferred to take his own, four-legged horse. But Odin warned him that he would need Sleipnir's help to reach the afterlife and return safely. For nine days and nine nights Hermod and Sleipnir rode towards Niflheim. Eventually, they arrived at the bridge over the river Gjoll, which separated the lands of the living from the land of the dead.

Sleipnir was about to gallop across when a woman leapt into their path. This was Mogdud, the guardian of the bridge. Sleipnir skidded to a halt on all eight of his legs. "This bridge," Mogdud said, "is only to be used by the dead. Have you come to the end of your life, Hermod?" Hermod was surprised she knew his name. "N–n–no. We are here to find my brother Baldr" he said nervously. Mogdud was silent for a moment. She remembered Baldr crossing the bridge a few days earlier.

Picture stone

This stone, carved some time between 700–900 CE, shows images from the Viking world, such as Sleipnir and other mythological characters, and a square-sailed Viking ship.

Hermod continued: "My mother has promised me all the love her heart can give if I bring Baldr back." Mogdud was stunned into silence. All the love a mother could give was the greatest prize she could imagine. She let Hermod and Sleipnir cross her bridge. They rode on, until eventually they came to the gates of Niflheim. The huge metal gates were so high that Hermod could not even see the top of them because they vanished into the mist. But they were no match for Sleipnir, who simply leapt with all of his eight legs over the top of them, as easily as if he was jumping over a fallen log. Odin had been right to tell Hermod to bring Sleipnir along on his journey.

The mist thickened and swirled around them as they made their way into Niflheim. Hermod was worried that he would not see clearly enough to recognise his brother. But he knew Baldr immediately. The brothers hugged tightly, although it was difficult to hug someone who had become more of a spirit than a human. Then the two of them found Hel, the guardian of the afterlife. They begged and pleaded with Hel, and Hermod told her that all of the gods and goddesses in Asgard were weeping and crying over the loss of Baldr. "In fact," Hermod continued, "there isn't a single person in the entire world who would not cry if they knew that Baldr had died." "Not a single person in the entire world?" Hel repeated. This seemed like a bold claim. "If every single person in the entire world cries for your brother, I will let you take him back to Asgard with you" she said. One by one, Hel summoned every last person and every creature in the world to her and told them how Baldr's brother had crossed the river of the dead to find him. And just as Hermod had said they would, each one of them left Niflheim in tears. Hel only managed to find one in the entire world who did not cry. She was a giant named Thokk, and she refused to cry for Baldr's death. "Let Hel keep what she has taken," the giant said, with a smirk.

Hermod had no problem crying. He had failed, and now Baldr would have to stay in Niflheim forever. But although Hel lived in the land of ice, her heart was not completely frozen. She could see how upset Hermod and Baldr were, so she offered the gods a compromise. "When the cockerel crows to mark the end of the world, I will return Baldr to you." It seemed like a long time to wait, but Hermod had no choice. He vowed that many lifetimes from now, when the end of the world came, he would go back down to Niflheim to fetch his long-lost brother.

BEASTS THAT FLY

Many ancient mythical beasts had magical powers. Those powers often reflected things that ancient humans could only dream of doing – like flying. In our modern world where we have built planes so that we can fly, it is difficult to imagine that humans dreamed of being able to do this. But the huge number of myths about beasts with wings that soar and swoop through the skies show that this was something that ancient people spent a lot of time thinking about.

The bird that swallowed the sun

A solar eclipse happens when the Moon moves between the Earth and the Sun, so that it becomes impossible to see the Sun from some parts of the Earth. Ancient people did not always know how to explain why solar eclipses happened. The ancient people who lived in what is now the Philippines came up with one possible explanation. They said that the Sun had been swallowed up by a giant creature who was part-dragon and part-bird. They called this creature Minokawa. In one ancient story told by Indigenous people, the bird's feathers are sharp like swords and its eyes reflect light like mirrors. The bird also ate the Moon, as well as the Sun, in some myths – and ancient people were afraid that it might also eat the Earth!

Odin's helpers

In Norse mythology, the god Odin is also called "the raven god". This is because he often appears accompanied by twin ravens called Huginn and Muninn. Their names mean 'thought' and 'memory' in the Old Norse language. These ravens flew all over the world, including to Midgard, the part of the world where the humans lived. They listened to the secrets of the humans and brought them back to Odin and the gods. Odin had given them the special ability to speak so that they could tell him everything they heard and saw.

This carving was broken off a bigger artwork, which showed both a Christian cross and a story from Viking mythology – Odin and one of his ravens battling a wolf called Fenrir.

The bird that created humans

In the mythology of the Kuku Yalunyu people of Far North Queensland, Australia, women were created by a magical bird. When the Earth was new, there were no women in the world. This was in a period called the Dreamtime, when the universe was being created. The Moon god, Gidja, thought that something was missing in the world. He made a wooden doll and put it inside of an eagle hawk called Yalungur. Then Gidja used magic to bring the wooden doll to life. Eventually, the doll was born a human and became the first woman.

The kalku becomes a chonchon

A kalku was a kind of sorcerer in old tales told by the Mapuche people, the Indigenous people whose homeland is in what is now Chile and Argentina. The kalku was known for making friends with dangerous spirits and monsters. They could fly, though it was not an easy process. First, they had to apply a magical potion to their throats. This would allow them to take their head off their neck. Then they would transform into a chonchon. Their ears would grow into wings – though they could only fly on nights when there was no Moon. They would grow feathers and claws so that they looked almost like a bird. No one knew that though, because humans could not see these creatures, even when they flew right past them.

Birds that come back to life

The phoenix is a bird that dies and is born again through a magical fire. In lots of different myths from around the ancient world, a bird that has special fire powers appears. The Firebird of ancient Slavic myth is an enormous bird with feathers that glow with red and orange light, like a fire. Even if they are plucked out of the bird, the feathers still shine brightly and can be used to light up a room. It is similar to the phoenix of Greek mythology, a bird that bursts into flames and then is born again into a new life. For the ancient Egyptians, a bird god called Bennu is a symbol of rebirth, and may have inspired the Greek phoenix. The Zulu people of Southern Africa tell an ancient story about an immortal firebird too. They call this bird the Lightning Bird, because it is able to summon lightning with its wings.

AZIZA AND THE SECRET SKILLS

Deep in the forest, under the ground, there lived Aziza, in a burrow between the roots of the silk-cotton tree. Humans had never laid eyes on Aziza. Creatures like Aziza were invisible to the human eye. But even though the humans could not see her, they never doubted that she was there. When the fruits started to ripen on the trees, as if by magic, the humans would say: "Aziza has helped us to eat again this year." And when the stars came out every night, the humans would thank Aziza for creating such beautiful artwork.

There were other things that Aziza and her family did for the humans that they did not know about. They would tie humans together with a tiny silver cord, so thin and delicate it could not be seen by humans or animals. The humans would feel connected to each other, but they had no idea what had connected them. They called this experience 'falling in love', because they could not see Aziza's tiny ropes. The humans could not see Aziza, or even hear her quiet whispers, but they knew that she could hear them. They knew this because when they got into trouble, they called on Aziza to help. In fact, that was how the humans had learned two of the most important skills that they knew.

Not many humans dared venture into the forest. There were elephants that could trample them to a pulp, and snakes with deadly venom. It was only when they were very hungry that they sent an unlucky hunter into the forest. The first hunter that year was a girl called Tassi. Like all who had gone before her, Tassi was reluctant. But people were starving. She had no choice but to try. Tassi thought of all the dangers ahead. She thought of what it would feel like to be trampled by an elephant, or bitten by a poisonous snake. But she did not make it far enough into the forest to meet any elephants or any snakes. She was so busy worrying that she forgot to watch her step. After only a hundred paces, she tripped over the branch and fell. Pain shot through her leg, but it was the least of her worries. She tried to stand but her leg could not hold her weight. It was broken, and now she had no way of ever getting out of the forest again.

"Aziza, if it really is true that you exist and that you use your powers to help humans, please help me!" Tassi begged quietly. Aziza heard the hunter's call. She flew out from her burrow underground and whispered instructions very quietly into Tassi's ear. Then Tassi, as if she had thought of it all on her own, broke off the branch of a nearby tree and tied it to her leg using the vines that were hanging over her head. Very carefully, she stood up and was able to walk just enough to get one hundred paces out of the forest and then shout for help to get her home to her village again. Aziza had told her about the right treatment for a broken leg – rest, and special herbs to help with swelling and bruises. Once her leg had healed, Tassi gave up hunting, which she never really liked, and used the special knowledge that Aziza had given her to help restore people to health.

The second hunter sent into the forest was named Gakpe. Gakpe could not speak, so when he found himself lost in the forest, much further than Tassi had ventured, he was unable to call on Aziza to help him. Aziza, though, did not need to be called. The truth was that she and her family always kept a watchful eye on the humans. So she knew when a human needed help without needing to be told. When Gakpe realised that he was lost and not going to be able to get home that night, he picked a fruit from the branches of one of the trees and was just about to eat it when something stopped him. Although he could not see what had happened, Aziza had fluttered up to him and whispered in his ear.

She had told him not to eat the fruit raw, but to make a fire by using a twig and a stone that lay on the ground in front of him. Gakpe, thinking that he had had this idea all on his own, did so. He placed pieces of wood one on top of the other, then struck the twig and the stone together until they sparked. To his amazement, he had made a fire, even though he had never done anything like that before. And when the fruit had cooked for a little while on the flame, he ate it.

Gakpe never knew that Aziza had saved him from death that day – the fruit was poisonous when eaten raw, but safe to eat when cooked. Gakpe returned to his village and he taught all of the other humans how to make a fire too, so that they could cook their food. Suddenly they realised there were many more things around them in the natural world that they could eat. All the other lessons the humans learned, they learned in the same way – with a few secret whispers from Aziza.

CREATURES OF THE AFTERLIFE

When ancient people thought about where they went after they had died, they imagined worlds full of mythical beasts. Some of these creatures were terrifying monsters who dragged wrongdoers to the underworld, while others represented a peaceful passing and gave comfort to those left behind. Either way, the journey to the afterlife was just as exciting and full of adventure as life itself.

The Furies

The terrifying Furies lived in the ancient Greek underworld. Their bodies were human except that they had bat wings and snakes for hair, and they barked like dogs. It was their job to take revenge. They were especially interested in mothers who had been wronged by their children. On hearing that a child lied to their mother the Furies would hunt them down and come up with the worst, most fitting punishment they could imagine.

This wooden mask is made in the shape of an animal the Dogon people know well, the hare. Hares can run very fast – among land animals they are second only to the cheetah, which also lives in Mali.

Dancing rabbit

In Mali, in West Africa, the Dogon people continue an ancient tradition by wearing animal masks. The ritual is performed after a person has died. People wear masks and perform dances. Some wear masks representing prey animals, like this one in the shape of a hare's head, and someone wears a mask of the hunter. In some communities, people will also wear masks in the shape of monkeys, lions, birds, and other animals. The hunter pretends to chase the animals away. These funeral rituals help the person who has died by chasing their spirit out of their body, out of the village, and into the afterlife.

Ereshkigal and the Gallu demons

Ereshkigal was the goddess of the ancient Mesopotamian underworld, which was called Kur. A family of demons called gallus lived alongside her in Kur. Their job was to drag unwilling people down into the land of the dead. One of the fiercest of these demons was called Asag. He was so terrifying that when he approached a river the water started to boil all of the fish, and even rocks and stones were afraid of him. Asag had three arms and three legs, and eyes all over his body. His skin felt hard and cold, like stone. He loved four things: making people sick, poisoning animals, drying up wells, and making people argue with each other for no good reason.

The four-eyed dogs and the bridge to death

In Zoroastrianism, an ancient religion still practiced in Iran, a bridge connects the land of the living to the land of the dead. It is guarded by two dogs, who have four eyes each. How the bridge looks depends on how the person who has died behaved in their lifetime. People who have been truthful will see a wide bridge that is easy to cross. People who have told lies will see a narrow bridge and struggle to balance their way across it. As they struggle, a demon will appear and will drag them down. Dogs are believed to keep evil away in Zoroastrianism. Some Zoroastrian funerals have a dog watching over the body of the dead person.

Swan of death

In Finnish mythology, the land of the dead is known as Tuonela. It is separated from the land of the living by a dark, wild, fast-flowing river, guarded by a black swan who makes sure that no one crosses before their time. The hero Lemminkäinen loved the daughter of the wicked queen Louhi. To stop him marrying her daughter, the queen gave him an impossible task: to kill the swan. Lemminkäinen waded into the water to catch the swan, but all of a sudden a whirlpool caught him and tore him into a thousand pieces.

The Devourer of Hearts

In ancient Egypt, Osiris was the god of the afterlife, which was called the Duat. Other gods lived there too, like Anubis, the jackal-headed god who guided souls to their fate. A beast called Ammit lived in the Duat. She had the head of a crocodile, and her body was part-lion and part-hippopotamus. Her special job was to swallow hearts. When the soul of a dead person entered the Duat, the Egyptians believed that their heart would be weighed. If the heart was lighter than a feather, then the person could pass into the Duat. If it weighed more than a feather, the soul would not pass the test. Their heart would be given to Ammit to devour.

THE WISE KITSUNE'S GIFT

The Kitsune always kept her promises. Once, when she was still a young fox, she snuck up to a man's table and stole his meal – but he caught her in the act. "If you let me keep your dinner," she said to him, "I will give you a gift that will make the lives of all humans better for the rest of time." It was too much for the man to resist. A better life for everyone for the rest of time? That was certainly worth more than a bowl of tofu and vegetables. He offered the bowl to the Kitsune. She ate it, then disappeared.

Fox netsuke
19th century

Just 3.5cm (1.5 inches), this carving is made to look like a mask worn to perform the role of Kitsune onstage, in a style of Japanese theatre called kyogen.

Back then, the Kitsune was still red in colour, just like any other fox. She had three tails, though she would go on to grow more tails over the years as her wisdom increased with age. Eventually, the Kitsune reached a thousand years old, and had grown her ninth tail, indicating that she had learnt all the wisdom that she was ever going to learn. The god of rice, who was called Inari, had changed the Kitsune's colour. Instead of red fur like other foxes, Inari gave her bright, golden fur.

It was at this stage in her life that the Kitsune began to think about the promise she had made to the man who had shared his meal with her all those years ago. It was time to keep it. She went to the town where the man lived. No one who lived there remembered the man any more, since a thousand

years had passed. But they knew of a creature called the Kitsune. They said that she had been seen flying through the air at night, or sending out lightning bolts. She had tried to walk among them as a woman but had failed to hide her tails. Everyone had heard that she had made a promise, and one day she would come back and bring them a gift that would improve their lives for the rest of time.

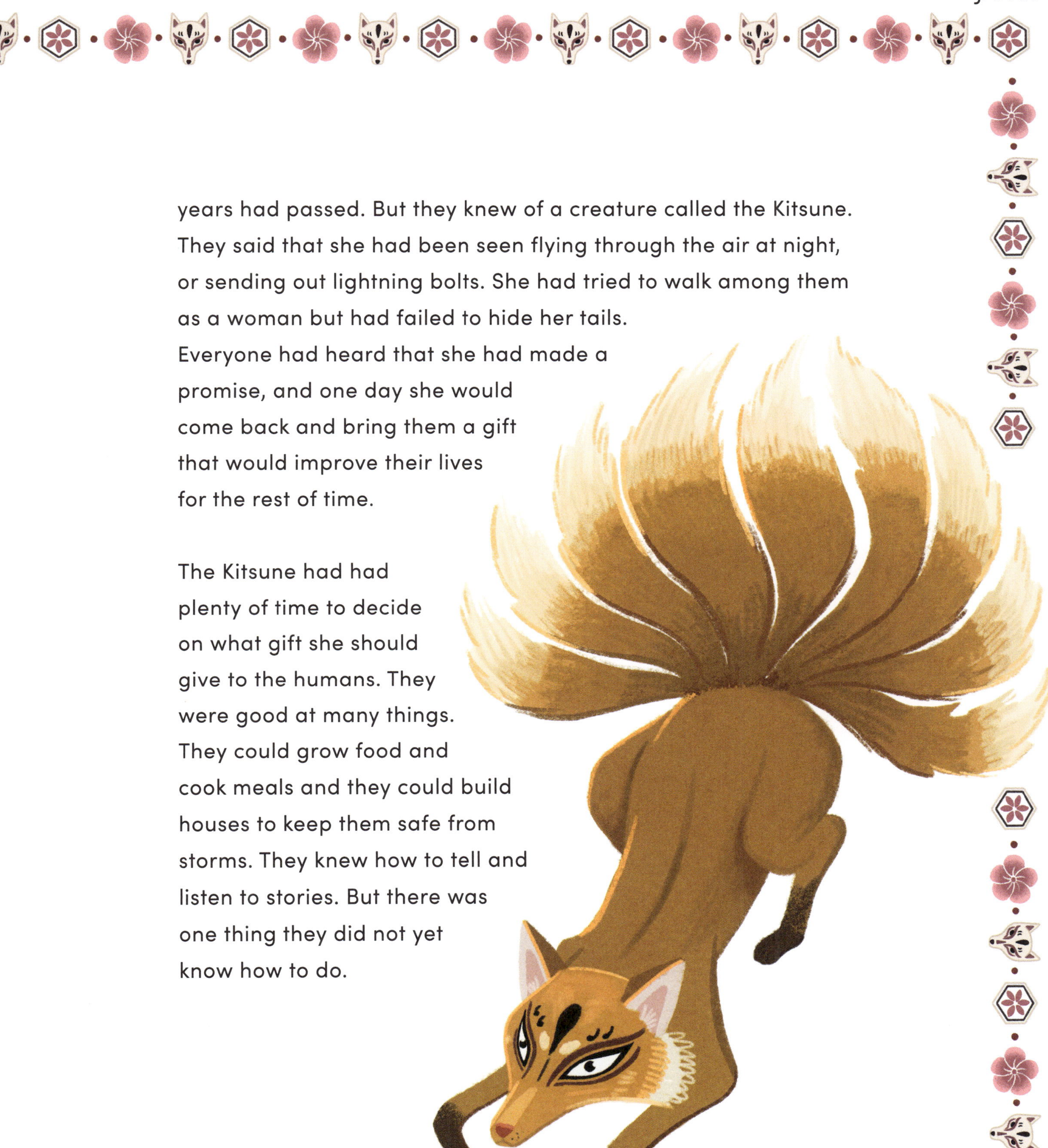

The Kitsune had had plenty of time to decide on what gift she should give to the humans. They were good at many things. They could grow food and cook meals and they could build houses to keep them safe from storms. They knew how to tell and listen to stories. But there was one thing they did not yet know how to do.

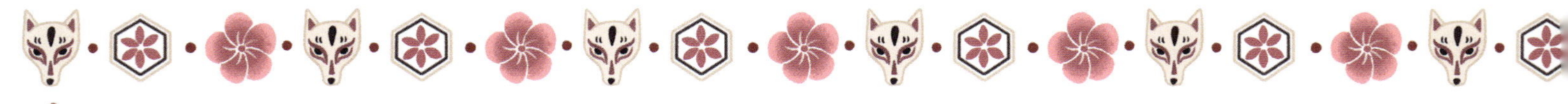

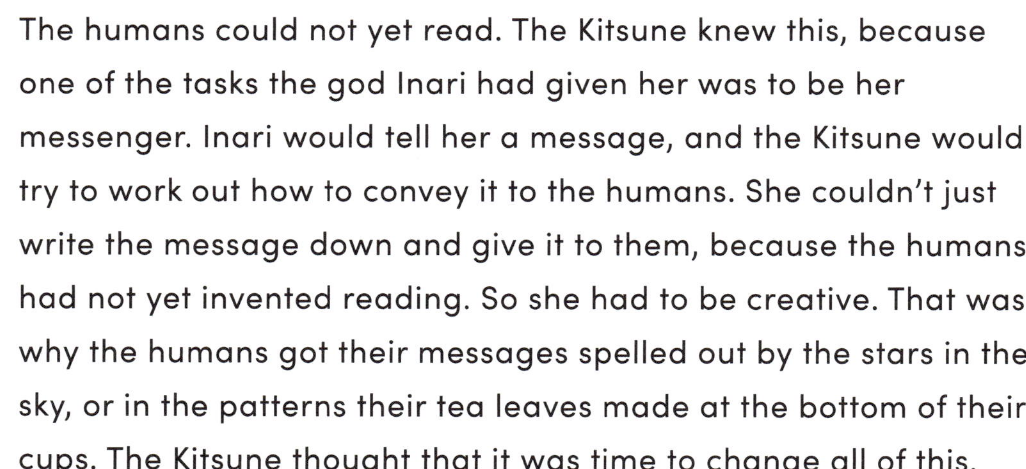

The humans could not yet read. The Kitsune knew this, because one of the tasks the god Inari had given her was to be her messenger. Inari would tell her a message, and the Kitsune would try to work out how to convey it to the humans. She couldn't just write the message down and give it to them, because the humans had not yet invented reading. So she had to be creative. That was why the humans got their messages spelled out by the stars in the sky, or in the patterns their tea leaves made at the bottom of their cups. The Kitsune thought that it was time to change all of this.

She swooped and soared across the night sky, until she came to the town where the kind man had once lived. She padded silently into a house where a girl named Fude and her family lived.
The Kitsune had chosen Fude specifically, because she was the kind of child who shared anything she had with others. The Kitsune was sure that Fude would share the special gift she was about to give her with all of the other children. She slipped into Fude's body, possessing her just like the stories about her said that she did.
The next morning when Fude woke up, she looked just like the little girl who had gone to sleep the night before, but she was actually possessed by the Kitsune. And the only way anyone could tell was if they saw the nine golden tails sticking out of her body.

Fude – or the Kitsune, since they were now one and the same – went to play with the other children that morning. She found that she could do something extraordinary. Dipping her fingers into the

dust on the ground, she could make markings. And what was more, she could read the markings aloud, and tell other people what they meant. Fude had learnt how to read. Letter by letter, she taught each of the other children how to read too. Soon it was not just letters that they could read, but whole words, sentences, and even stories.

Eventually – after having a lot of fun living among the humans and learning a few new skills herself – the Kitsune left Fude's body. By then, the humans could never forget the magical skill that they had learnt. Now, when she needed to convey messages to them, the Kitsune (and all of the messengers of the gods who came after her) could simply write to the humans. And they could write down their stories and memories and songs, so that they would never forget them.

It was true what the Kitsune had said – her gift had given the humans a better life for the rest of time.

WHY DO WE BELIEVE IN MONSTERS?

Stories about mythical beasts are all around us. Monsters find us, even when we are not looking for them. Sometimes we can spot them in the words of people who care about us and don't want us to get hurt. "Don't go into the forest at night, or a monster will get you!" someone will say, or "It's dangerous to swim too far out from the shore, because an enormous beast lives there!" These warnings are actually stories. There are monsters lurking in each of them. But more importantly, there is something else: the love of the person telling the story. Mythical beasts are a shape that we give to dangers we want to protect other people from.

The strange thing about myths is that they do not need to have actually happened in order to tell us the truth. We don't meet monsters in our everyday lives. But they do represent real feelings. They show us our real fears. And this is a very important job. Without mythical beasts it would be much more difficult for us humans to talk about the things we are scared of.

Mythical beasts in stories are often deliberately described as terrifying creatures. They have sharp claws, long teeth, or horns on their heads. We are told that they can breathe fire, or sting us with poisonous tails, or swallow us up before we have even noticed that they are there. But the most important thing about these monsters is not what they look like, but what they stand for: real dangers like deep water, or being alone in the dark.

When people in the ancient world gathered together over a meal, or while they were out at work, they told each other stories about monsters, beasts, and other mythical creatures. Sometimes these stories were warnings. Sometimes they were stories that reminded us how much we needed each other, and how important it is to treat others fairly.

As I have been piecing these stories together, I have learnt something about what we are afraid of. I have learnt that humans, wherever they are from and wherever they live, share many of our fears: the fear that we might damage the Earth, that children might be lost, that we might be alone. We are more similar in what scares us than we might think. Stories about mythical beasts can do other things than scare us, of course. They can show us the power of the natural world, and how much better it is to work with nature than against it. Other stories tell us about unlikely friendships and about all the times we turned out to be wrong in our assumptions. But the most common job that monsters do is help us talk about what scares us.

Fear is a very strange thing. It's something we don't often get the chance to talk about, even though we might want to. "I'm not scared!" we say, even when we are. Stories about mythical beasts are our chance to admit to each other that there are things that we are scared of – that we are all scared of. And being able to admit this gives us an opportunity to face these fears. Some of them we will be able to conquer. Others we will simply learn to live with. Some of them will require us to change everything about the way the world works. But it is only by working together that we will be able to face them.

INDEX

E

F

G

H

I

J

ACKNOWLEDGEMENTS

The publisher would like to thank the following people for their assistance:
Rica Dearman for proofreading; Helen Peters for the index.

The publisher would like to thank the following for their kind permission to reproduce their photographs:

(Key: a-above; b-below/bottom; c-centre; f-far; l-left; r-right; t-top)

1 Alamy Stock Photo: Peter Horree (c). **19 Bridgeman Images:** Giancarlo Costa (crb). **20 © The Trustees of the British Museum. All rights reserved:** (cra). **The Metropolitan Museum of Art:** Rogers Fund, 1941 (crb). **21 Alamy Stock Photo:** Peter Horree (tl). **23 Bridgeman Images:** NPL - DeA Picture Library / S. Vannini (cra). **26 The Metropolitan Museum of Art:** Gift of Norbert Schimmel Trust, 1989 (tr). **27 © The Trustees of the British Museum. All rights reserved:** (cl). **The Metropolitan Museum of Art:** Gift of Theodore M. Davis, 1907 (07.226.1) (br). **28 Alamy Stock Photo:** World History Archive (cr). **Dorling Kindersley**: Jerry Young (br). **29 The Metropolitan Museum of Art:** Gift of Lily S. Place, 1923 (tl); Gift of Edward S. Harkness, 1917 (cr). **36 The Metropolitan Museum of Art:** The Crosby Brown Collection of Musical Instruments, 1889 (clb). **40 © The Trustees of the British Museum. All rights reserved:** (tl). **45 Alamy Stock Photo:** Yogi Black (crb). **51 Bridgeman Images:** (tr). **52 The Metropolitan Museum of Art:** Gift of J. Pierpont Morgan, 1917 (cra). **53 The Metropolitan Museum of Art:** Rogers Fund, 1985 (cla). **62 Harvard Art Museums:** President and Fellows of Harvard College (tr). **The Metropolitan Museum of Art:** The Michael C. Rockefeller Memorial Collection, Bequest of Nelson A. Rockefeller, 1979 (bc). **63 The Metropolitan Museum of Art:** Purchase, Joseph Pulitzer Bequest, 1966 (br). **68 The Metropolitan Museum of Art:** Rogers Fund, 1943 (clb). **69 Bridgeman Images:** Godong (bl). **71 © The Trustees of the British Museum. All rights reserved:** (bc). **74 The Metropolitan Museum of Art:** Gift of Judith Riklis, 1983 (tr); Rogers Fund, 1964 (br). **75 The Metropolitan Museum of Art:** Gift of Margaret B. Zorach, 1980 (cl). **83 Bridgeman Images:** 2023 Museum of Fine Arts, Boston. All rights reserved. / Museum purchase with funds donated in honor of Edward W. Forbes (tr); Christie's Images (bl). **88 The Metropolitan Museum of Art:** Edith Perry Chapman Fund, 1966 (bc); Gift of Theodore M. Davis, 1914 (tr). **89 The Metropolitan Museum of Art**: Purchase, Rogers Fund and Anonymous Gift, 1979 (cla). **91 Alamy Stock Photo:** LMA / AW (tr). **98 Bridgeman Images:** Luisa Ricciarini (tr). **The Metropolitan Museum of Art:** Gift of Jonathan and Jeannette Rosen, 2015 (bl); Purchase, Anonymous Gift and Rogers Fund, 1978 (crb). **99 Alamy Stock Photo:** Pictures From History / CPA Media Pte Ltd (bl, bc). **102 Bridgeman Images:** Freer Sackler Gallery / Gift of Arthur M. Sackler (tl). **109 Bridgeman Images:** (tr). **110 Alamy Stock Photo:** World History Archive (tr). **111 Bridgeman Images:** Lowe Art Museum / Museum purchase through funds from Beaux Arts (tc). **113 Dreamstime.com:** Pius Lee (tr). **116 Bridgeman Images:** Photo Josse (cr). **117 Bridgeman Images:** G. Dagli Orti / © NPL - DeA Picture Library (br). **124 Alamy Stock Photo:** World History Archive (tl). **126 Bridgeman Images:** Manx National Heritage (bc). **126-127 Dreamstime.com:** Tatiana Mezhenina (Background). **127 Dreamstime.com:** Aussiesnakes (cla). **132 Bridgeman Images:** NPL - DeA Picture Library (tr). **133 Bridgeman Images:** (crb). **134 The Metropolitan Museum of Art:** Gift of Mrs. Russell Sage, 1910 (cl)